CONTEMPORARY
WORSHIP SERVICES

By James L. Christensen

Funeral Services
The Minister's Service Handbook
The Minister's Marriage Handbook
The Complete Funeral Manual
Contemporary Worship Services

CONTEMPORARY
WORSHIP SERVICES
A Sourcebook

JAMES L. CHRISTENSEN

FLEMING H. REVELL COMPANY
Old Tappan, New Jersey

CONTENTS

8 CONTENTS

Section 3 SERMONS: SUCCESSFUL EXPERIMENTS

Section 4 MUSIC SOURCES

INTRODUCTION

My niece, typical of many youth, had never really been "turned on" by traditional worship, though she attended church because her mother did. Not until she began attending the contemporary services at a local church while a student at the university did worship seem to capture her interest. "It seemed to speak to me," she excitingly related to her uncle minister. "I became involved, and actually looked forward eagerly to Sunday. It conveyed a depth of meaning and faith on my level of experience."

This and other similar testimonies on the part of my own teenage daughters and other youth has caused me to experiment and develop materials with a more contemporary flavor. "If this is what youth and young adults will respond to," I reasoned, "then I must open-mindedly try it because approximately 50 percent of the population is under twenty-five. Certainly the church has not been communicating adequately to this segment of the population." This book is the result of some of my efforts to produce and accumulate usable contemporary materials.

"What is it about the contemporary service that is appealing?" I asked myself. The contemporary service seems important for some of the following reasons.

First, it attempts to meet people where they are in scientific understanding, with a vocabulary that expresses faith in terms relevant to the twentieth-century mind. Relevancy is the crucial issue which dominates every aspect of Christianity today. It may be true that too often the worship and teaching experiences of the church are artificial, suspended in a world nobody knows. This is why from time to time worship materials may be legitimately restudied and hopefully recast in contemporary coinage.

Contemporary worship strives to use contemporary thought forms and urban language rather than ancient myths and rural language; terms of city planners, not shepherds, psychological insights, not demons. The Second Vatican Council after persistent lay demands, updated the mass in an understandable language of the age. So contemporary worship attempts to make the experience meaningful to the average person in the pew.

Second, contemporary worship attempts to recapture the spirit of celebration, expressing joy in what the Holy Spirit has done and is doing in the world. Themes of worship focus on the new life and victory in Christ's love and hope. This mood is created by the tempo of music used, the festal use of banners, by symbols and colors, and content of materials. Dull, dead, dry, sleepy, mournful, repetitious services have characterized too much worship.

Third, contemporary worship is oriented to the needs of persons, rather than the needs of the institution. Some traditional worship services have seemed tantamount to a rally encouraging support and loyalty to the organization. Contemporary worship is sensitive to the feelings and aspirations of the worshipers. Whereas traditional worship has been focused upon God's transcendence above and apart from creation, contemporary worship focuses upon where God intersects humanity in everyday happenings. In worldly realities we find God and are found by Him. The major emphasis of most contemporary services is upon God's judgment, reconciliation and mission.

Furthermore, contemporary worship strives to involve the worshiper in the process, by participation, both bodily and mentally. Traditionally, the altar has been far from the people, elevated and behind a special enclosure designed to keep the altar at a distance. The chancel is where the minister and choir are placed, separated, elevated, and dramatically spotlighted appearing as "on stage." The obvious conclusion has been that the "real thing was taking place up there" while congregations are passive spectators. The farther back you can sit, the more "out of it" you are.

The effectiveness depends upon how professional the choir and minister perform. The new departure is an attempt to make an entire worshiping community, re-enacting the drama of life and salvation. Worship in its true sense is more than watching a show led by the minister, or hearing a production, though many attender at the traditional service is more of a spectator than participant. Ideally, each person is to be in the process, confronted with personal decision. This the contemporary service strives to accomplish.

Contemporary worship, likewise, is characterized by a focus upon life and the social applications of faith, in contrast to the other-worldly emphasis. A basic premise is the view that the church is servant, and a leaven in the world. The Christian lives in a secular world and contemporary worship trains the Christian for witness in such a responsibility.

To accomplish these purposes, contemporary worship utilizes new forms, modern ballads, varied instruments, light, color, all kinds of arts, movements, dance, recorded music, films, picture projections, clapping, Scriptures and prayers with words that are in current usage, and varied sermon methods. Popular music usually accompanied by guitars and ukuleles, and occasionally trumpet, drums, vibra-harp or accordion is typical of most modernized services.

Varied environments are accomplished by changing lights, artificially controlled with rheostats and mirrors, and photographs shown rapidly upon a screen. The potential values in the use of lights are only partially realized. There is likewise a great treasury of colors and shapes, for what worshipers see is as important as what they hear. Consciousness is also expanded by bodily movement accomplished in interpretive ballet.

One of the most apparent and necessary innovations of the contemporary service is the translation and paraphrasing of Christian traditions, Scriptures and prayer into words of daily vocabulary and modern images and idioms. Much of Christian tradition is in archaic language. Contemporary worship seeks to make the language of worship the language of life.

Now these innovations may shock and excite many tradition-oriented members. Therefore, the worship leader must keep balance and avoid extremes as a regular diet. If he is steeped only in the traditional forms of worship, he risks being irrelevant to the twentieth-century mind. On the other hand, if he is extremely far-out he risks losing the historical perspective and the tradition-oriented segment of the congregation. Both results are unfortunate, and to be avoided if possible.

This note of warning needs to be sounded. At a time when liturgy is in a state of ferment and experiment and development, we must not sacrifice the essential psychological and theological aspects of worship in the desire to be contemporary. Always worship should be more God-centered than man-centered, more objective than subjective. Praise, confession, absolution, instruction, offering of self and dedication are indispensable aspects of worship whether it be traditional or contemporary.

I am suggesting that it is possible to orient a congregation to appreciate the contemporary service that is done in good taste and order. It would not be wise to replace entirely, or suddenly, if ever, the traditional services. Perhaps an occasional complete contemporary service with youth participating and for which the congregation is properly prepared is the better way to begin. Several special seasons afford such an opportunity for which materials are here included.

Or again, it is possible to utilize some new forms, new vocabulary, new readings as inclusions in a part of the regular traditional services. These, too, are included within these pages. Hopefully, these materials may be of value to other clergymen such as myself.

JAMES L. CHRISTENSEN

CONTEMPORARY
WORSHIP SERVICES

Section 1

SERVICES FOR
TODAY'S CHRISTIAN

Experimental Sanctuary Services

Dramatic Worship Celebrations

Small Group Experiments

Contemporary Wedding Ceremonies

Modern Funeral Service

CELEBRATION OF OUR GATHERING

As We Gather (*instrumental ensemble*) "The Spirit Is A' Movin'," "Go Tell It on the Mountain," "Thank You, Jesus"

We Welcome One Another

LEADER Welcome to another week of life.

PEOPLE In gratitude we come to celebrate because we are alive.

LEADER We are here because God is the Giver and Provider of all life.

PEOPLE We are here to acknowledge Him, to remember our heritage, and to try to be the people He intended.

We Join Together (*in unison*) O Creator of all that is and is to be; we bow to confess our illusions, pride, hostility, prejudices and greed which are the roots of the larger problems. O Lord, have mercy upon us and forgive us.

We Sing Together "Prayer for Mercy"

We Lift Our Voices "Praise God, Hurray"

TEACH US OF LIFE

LEADER (*from the New Testament,* "The Sacrificial Life") Anyone who wishes to be a follower of mine, said Jesus, must leave self behind; he must assume a sacrificial life and come with me. Whoever cares for his own safety will be lost in frustration, but if a person will let himself go for my sake, and for the truth, he will find the real security and what is more, inner peace. What does a person really gain by winning the whole world, if by so doing he loses his true self? You can never buy your true self back once it is bartered away.

17

(*from the NOW Testament,* "The Waiting World") This world waits for you! Oh, no! It won't do to say you don't count! This world longs for anyone who will lift instead of lean, who will love instead of hate, who will help instead of hinder. You do count! If this weeping world is ever to be a better and more loving place, it will be up to you. Whether you despise it, or love it, or ignore it, or even know it, this world is waiting.

CHORAL GROUP   "What Will I Do?"

TELL US OF LIFE

LEADER (*sermon*)   "Filling Your Years With Life" (*Invitation for congregational response with opportunity for questions: ten minutes*)

TRIGGER US FOR LIFE

We Pray (*spontaneous prayers from worshipers*)

We Give Our Money (*offering collection*)

We Give Ourselves (*hymn*)   "All That I Am I Give to Thee"

CELEBRATE OUR SCATTERING

PEOPLE   "Go Tell It on the Mountain" (*song*)
LEADER   Shalom!
PEOPLE   Shalom!

CELEBRATION IN THANKSGIVING

The Preparation
CELEBRANT   Let us worship God.
ORGAN (*prelude*)   "Now Thank We All Our God" (Karg-Elert)

ALL (*processional hymn*) "Today Is The Day" (Neil Blunt)

CELEBRANT We are here.

PEOPLE In the name of Jesus Christ.

ALL We are here because we are man, but often we deny our humanity. We do not love others as we should. We hide from each other and from our true selves. We war against life. We hurt each other. We are sorry for it, and we are sick from it. We seek new life.

CELEBRANT Giver of life, heal us and free us to be true human beings.

ALL Holy Spirit, speak to us. Help us to listen for we are very deaf. Come, fill us this moment.

SINGER (*response*) "O Lamb of God"

CELEBRANT We confess that we complain when we cannot get second helpings or dessert.

ALL O Lord, bless with better nourishment those who do not know the taste of meat.

CELEBRANT We complain about the lack of variety, and are fussy when it isn't cooked to our liking or seasoned properly.

ALL O Lord, show love to those who have only rice, who drink from muddy waters and know no modern appliances.

CELEBRANT We claim we are not able to live on $1.65 an hour.

ALL Lord, pity those who barely exist and hasten greater justice and distribution of the earth's produce.

CELEBRANT We complain about the high cost of medicine and doctors.

ALL O Lord, burden us with the fact that many people die without any medical care in their lives.

CELEBRANT The room is too hot, or too cold—we cannot sleep in our soft well-mattressed beds.

ALL Lord, grant rest to those who must sleep in the gutters, who have no place to lay their heads.

CELEBRANT Is there a reason for this inequality?

ALL O Lord, look upon all our abundance. Forgive us for our

ingratitude, grant us concern and unselfishness that we may humble ourselves, and help those less fortunate than we.

SINGER (*response*) "Hear Our Prayer, O Lord"

THE SERVICE OF THE WORD

READER (*the Old Testament lesson*) Psalm 100 paraphrased (*See elsewhere in the book.*)

SINGER (*response*) "*Gloria in Excelsis*" (Glory to God in the Highest)

READER (*the New Testament lesson*) Philippians 4:4–9

SINGER (*response*) "O Sons and Daughters"

MINISTER (*the proclamation of the word*) "The Attitude of Gratitude"

SINGER (*response*) "That's for Me"

THE SERVICE OF OFFERING AND THANKSGIVING

Thanksgiving for the World of Things

CELEBRANT We revel, O God, for the wonder of the universe which You have made our home.

ALL For air and water; for darkness and light; for gravity and relativity; for green plants and grass, and trees that shelter birds that sing, for all that we see and what we do not—we give thanks.

CELEBRANT We are appreciative of all that is beautiful.

ALL For summer clouds and soft blue sky; for tall straight trees and warm friendly puppies that meet us at the door; for daytime and nighttime; for the moon and stars, for everything, we give thanks.

Thanksgiving for the World of People

CELEBRANT We thank God for people in general.

ALL For people who have understanding of life and its true meaning, and teach the same to others; for people who serve personal needs unselfishly and humbly; for people who bring beauty and joy into the world; for people who do the best they can; for people who are respectful of those who differ with them; for people who seek the truth, and are careful in protecting the good name of others; for people who love even the unlovely.

Thanksgiving for God

CELEBRANT We thank God for Himself.

ALL We thank Him for His love, which we can never deserve but without which we could never survive.

CELEBRANT We thank Him for giving us hearts and minds that can be satisfied ultimately only by truth.

ALL We thank Him for giving us free wills that give dignity to our lives and responsibility.

CELEBRANT We thank Him for the glorious privilege of being partners with Him in completing His creation and establishing righteousness and love among men.

ALL We thank Him that when there seems to be no conceivable help, there is help beyond our physical powers.

CELEBRANT We rejoice in life and acknowledge our thanks by giving our time, money and life.

ALL In the glory of life, we give.

The Offering

SINGERS "The Lord's Prayer" followed by the "Doxology" (*as offering is taken to altar*).

CELEBRANT Let us pass the peace my friends. (The gift of peace is passed from one person to another, saying, "The peace of God be with you." The response is, "And with you.")

ALL (*hymn*) "I've Found Your Love In This Place"

FREEDOM AND DEMOCRACY SUNDAY

Prelude

INSTRUMENTALISTS (*processional hymn*)   "God of Our Fathers," (*traditional, with trumpets and timpani; two Boy Scouts present the colors: the American and Christian flags*)

ALL (*American flag salute*) (*unison*)

ALL (*Christian flag salute*) (*unison*)   I pledge allegiance to the Christian flag and to the Saviour for whose Kingdom it stands —one brotherhood, uniting all mankind in service and in love.

LEADER (*invocation*)   Kind Providence: We are glad we live in America where we are free to choose our occupations, our leaders, our life style; to speak our mind and to live according to our own religious scruples. We acknowledge the paradox, however, that only in servitude to Jesus Christ are we truly free. So commit us to use our freedom to be our best and not our worst in the Spirit of Jesus Christ, Amen.

LEADER   The birthright of every American is freedom. As the Preamble to the Constitution reads:

We the people of the United States, in order to form a more perfect Union, establish justice, insure domestic tranquility, provide for the common defense, promote the general welfare, and secure the blessings of liberty to ourselves and our posterity, do ordain and establish this Constitution for the United States of America.

ALL (*contemporary hymn*)   "Born Free"

SPEAKING CHORUS   Choral—"I Am the Nation" by Otto Whittaker (*lights dim with spot on flag*)

I was born on July 4, 1776, and the Declaration of Independence is my birth certificate. The bloodlines of the world run in my veins, because I offered freedom to the oppressed. I am many things, and many people. **I AM THE NATION.**

I am 200 million living souls—and the ghost of millions who have lived and died for me.

I am Nathan Hale and Paul Revere. I stood at Lexington and fired the shot heard around the world. I am Washington, Jefferson, and Patrick Henry. I am John Paul Jones, the Green Mountain boys, and Davy Crockett. I am Lee, Grant, and Abe Lincoln.

I remember the Alamo, the *Maine*, and Pearl Harbor. When freedom called, I answered and stayed until it was over, over there. I left my heroic dead in Flanders Fields, on the rock of Corregidor, on the bleak slopes of Korea and in the steaming jungle of Vietnam.

I am the Brooklyn Bridge, the wheat lands of Kansas, and the granite hills of Vermont. I am the coal fields of the Virginias and Pennsylvania, the fertile lands of the West, the Golden Gate and the Grand Canyon. I am Independence Hall, the *Monitor* and the *Merrimac*.

I am big. I sprawl from the Atlantic to the Pacific . . . my arms reach out to embrace Alaska and Hawaii . . . three million square miles throbbing with industry. I am more than three million farms. I am forest, field, mountain and desert. I am quiet villages in the country—and teeming cities that never sleep.

You can look at me and see Ben Franklin walking down the streets of Philadelphia with his breadloaf under his arm. You can see Betsy Ross with her needle. You can see the lights of Christmas, and hear the strains of "Auld Lang Syne" as the calendar turns.

I am Babe Ruth and the World Series. I am 130,000 schools and colleges, and 326,000 churches where my people worship God as they think best. I am a ballot dropped in a box, the roar of a crowd in a stadium, and the voice of a choir in a cathedral. I am an editorial in a newspaper and a letter to a Congressman.

I am Eli Whitney and Stephen Foster. I am Tom Edison, Albert Einstein, and Billy Graham. I am Horace Greeley, Will Rogers, and the Wright Brothers. I am George Washington Carver, Daniel Webster, and Jonas Salk.

I am Longfellow, Harriet Beecher Stowe, Walt Whitman, and Thomas Paine.

Yes, I am the nation, and these are the things that I am. I was conceived in freedom and, God willing, in freedom will I spend the rest of my days.

May I possess always the integrity, the courage and the strength to keep myself unshackled, to remain a citadel of freedom and a beacon of hope to the world.

I AM THE UNITED STATES.

ALL (*anthem*) "Give Me Your Tired, Your Poor. . . ."

LEADER   And what is the future of our nation? It has been torn with racial tension, injustice, demonstrations—perhaps these are purposeful in making us a better people—a nation for all people.

As dark and foreboding as it appears, yet there are rays on the horizon.

Thomas Wolfe articulates our faith in saying, "I think the true discovery of America is before us. I think the true fulfillment of our spirit, of our people, of our mighty and immortal land, is yet to come. I think the true discovery of our own democracy is still before us. And I think that all these things are certain as the morning, as inevitable as noon. I think I speak for most men living when I say that our America is Here, is Now, and beckons on before us, and that this glorious assurance is not only our living hope, but our dream to be accomplished."

ALL (*closing hymn*) "Battle Hymn of the Republic"

LEADER (*benediction*) Go now, remembering that you are free —by God's good favor. May you be responsible and obedient wherever you are—and the peace and joy of God be with you. Amen.

BROTHERHOOD SUNDAY

LEADER   Come let us experience God's community.

ALL (*unison affirmation*)   It is the human community that is the focus of our religious life, not as spectator, but as both actor and stage of the drama of our worship. The center of our concern is man, not in the abstract, but man in his most concrete and whole life in the real and often ambiguous world. We seek to celebrate life—in action and reflection; to seek and to celebrate what it means to be persons in community under the God we know in Jesus Christ. We affirm the right of each person to seek his own way by his own lights, yet seek it in a mutuality of trust and concern.

ALL (*hymn*)   "Let's Get Together"

LEADER   Our Father, who art in heaven. . . .

ALL (*response*)   You are the ground of our being, the soil from which personality has blossomed. Purity and truth, justice and love spring from You. In You we are kin to every person.

LEADER   Hallowed be Thy name. . . .

ALL (*response*)   We speak reverently Your name, and humble ourselves in admiration, appreciation and dependence.

LEADER   Thy kingdom come on earth. . . .

ALL (*response*)   How long, O God? How long? Above all our selfish goals and aspirations, help us to yearn and dream, pray and work for brotherhood among men. Amid the disorder and violence, hasten the day, O Lord, through sensitive servants.

LEADER   Give us this day our daily bread. . . .

ALL (*response*)   Not for tomorrow and its needs, but for this day's responsibilities, provide us wisdom and strength, we pray, believing that if we fill this day with quality and live this day to its best, we can trust ample care of our future. Wherever and whatever be our condition, save us from worry.

LEADER   Forgive us our sins as we forgive those who sin against us. . . .

ALL (*response*)   You have shown us Your forgiveness of us in Christ. Even in our enmity, and in spite of our littleness, You have forgiven. Help us to not withhold mercy and love to those who abuse us, for in going the second mile and in forgiving seventy times seven, we find the barriers melting down and reconciliation effected. In the power of love is the hope of our fractured world. O God, answer our Saviour's prayer through and in us.

LEADER   Lead us not into temptation. . . .

ALL (*response*)   Keep us from the influences which would degrade us, or cause us to be less than our best.

ALL   For Thine is the Kingdom and the Power and the Glory forever. Amen.

CHORAL READING   "No One Asked" (*See* Section 4)

Responsive Prayer of Confession

LEADER   Let us confess our sin in the polarization of society.

ALL   Loving Heavenly Father, look at us in our separation from You, our neighbors, and ourselves.

LEFT SIDE   In our arrogance and error we have divided men.

RIGHT SIDE   We have called some "sinners" and others "righteous."

LEFT   But we as men know that we are all sinners.

RIGHT   We realize how strange we are to each other.

LEFT   And how estranged life is from life.

RIGHT   Each of us draws back unto himself.

LEFT   Sometimes we take secret joy in the misfortune of our best friends.

RIGHT   But we are dishonest enough to deny that this is true.

LEFT   We have consistently mistrusted others.

RIGHT   Assuming the other is seeking to serve himself even if it means betraying us,

LEFT   We question his motives,

RIGHT   Taking it for granted he does not really care.

LEFT   We, on our part, have often been unworthy of trust . . .

RIGHT   We have not accepted our neighbor as he is.

LEFT   We have kept the right to reject the black if he does not meet us on our terms.

RIGHT   In all these acts and in our attitudes, we have refused to risk the chance that we shall not be loved in return.

LEFT   Or the possibility that someone may think us fools for exposing our hearts,

RIGHT   Or the probability that we will fail or be failed against, and that there will be pain.

ALL   We therefore seek Your forgiveness, that we might be one with each other and with You. Amen.

(*silence*)

Words of Acceptance

LEADER   You are accepted as you now are, timid in your love but aware of your timidity, afraid really to trust those with whom you worship, yet willing to try. Thus God, the *only* One, without whose forgiveness you cannot be reborn to new courage and trust and love, sees directly through your eyes into your heart. His unqualified word to us is just this: "I love you, now and always." Amen.

ALL   Amen!

Words of Covenant

LEFT SIDE   We are the brotherhood of men.

RIGHT SIDE   We are together the Body of Christ.

LEFT   Trust my love.

RIGHT   Trust my love.

LEFT   I do trust your love, and accept it.

RIGHT   I do trust your love, and accept it. Amen.

LEFT   Amen.

ALL (*hymn*) "We Are One in the Spirit" (*As song is sung, a circle will be formed around sanctuary, with everyone interlocking arms, forming a human chain.*)

LEADER (*benediction*) (*congregation repeating phrase by phrase after minister*) Let us, by our acts of love/ break down the barriers/ that would otherwise become stumbling blocks/ to the lives of our neighbors./ Let us together in the spirit of Christ/ become closer and in one purpose/ work together in kinship/ upholding each man's dignity/ to the end that God's Kingdom of right relationships/ might come on earth. Amen.

ALL (*song response*) "Shalom"

WORLD ORDER SUNDAY

Instrumental Prelude (*guitars, drums, etc.*)

Litany of Greeting

LEADER Good morning, my friends!

PEOPLE Good morning to you!

LEADER Let us come together in that which could unite us all:

PEOPLE The Spirit of our Lord, Jesus the Christ.

LEADER Let us remember that we have been chosen by God.

PEOPLE Chosen to be His servants in our world.

LEADER Remember that we come together because of our common need for renewal.

PEOPLE Let us worship God in such a way that He is able to renew us for and in His service.

LEADER Grace to you and peace from God the Father and His son, our Lord Jesus Christ.

ALL Amen.

ALL (*song of gathering*)   "Sons of God"
READER   Psalm 146 paraphrased

> Praise the Lord, brothers and sisters, Praise the Lord!
> Praise the Lord God all your life long!
> Sing to Him as long as you live.
>
> Have no hope in anything less.
> No hope in power, no hope in human ways,
> To make you unfree and a slave to what exists.
>
> He it is, brothers and sisters, He it is,
> Who has the power to make the blind see,
> Health for the sick and food for the hungry.
>
> He it is, brothers and sisters, He it is,
> So perfect in justice, frees us from our sins,
> Makes us restless for the building of new worlds.
>
> All else that beckons to our hope must surely die,
> Must yield its breath, return to helpless dust,
> Only the Lord God remains completely free.[1]

PEOPLE   Happy is the man whose hope is strong, whose hope is fixed on the Lord our God.

PEOPLE (*song*)   "He's Got the Whole World In His Hands"

READER (*prayer of confession*)

> For lack of hope
> For our yielding to despair
> For our complacency and fear of change
> For being satisfied with the way things are
> For the trust we put in war and violence
> For the trust we put in wealth and property
> For the trust we put in everything conventional
> For our failure to be signs of hope
> For the fragility of our faith and hope in you.

PEOPLE   Lord, have mercy upon us. O God, have mercy and forgive us.

MINISTER (*reading of scriptures*)   I Corinthian: 13 (modernized—*see* Section 2)

Prayers of Petition

CONGREGATION   O God, Your ways are higher than our ways, and Your thoughts greater than ours; we humbly invoke Your guidance and spirit.

LEFT SIDE   With students and faculty becoming pitted against university administrators and political leaders of the state and nation . . .

RIGHT SIDE   Help us to understand both sides and to actively work as agents of reconciliation between them.

LEFT   With conservatives and liberals alienated, and the gaps between youth and parents, black and white, labor and management, poor and comfortable growing into violence,

RIGHT   Help us to understand and to actively work as agents of reconciliation between them.

LEFT   With those who want radical change within the community and the church and with those who wish to retain the status quo and to keep the church as it has always been in the past

RIGHT   Help us to understand and to actively work as agents of reconciliation.

LEFT   With our family and friends where misunderstandings frequently occur

RIGHT   Give us the grace to be more understanding and to reconcile our own life to Christlikeness. Amen.

PEOPLE (*song*)   "Our Lives Free From Sin"

MINISTER (*sermon*)   "Divided We Stand"

PEOPLE (*song*)   "In Christ, There Is No East or West"

ALL (*Read preamble to Charter of United Nations*)

WE THE PEOPLES
OF THE UNITED NATIONS
DETERMINED

to save succeeding generations from the scourge of war, which twice in our lifetime has brought untold sorrow to mankind, and

to reaffirm faith in fundamental human rights, in the dignity and worth of the human person, in the equal rights of men and women and of nations large and small, and to establish conditions under which justice and respect for the obligations arising from treaties and other sources of international law can be maintained, and

to promote social progress and better standards of life in larger freedom,

AND FOR THESE ENDS

to practice tolerance and live together in peace with one another as good neighbors, and

to unite our strength to maintain international peace and security, and

to ensure, by the acceptance of principles and the institution of methods, that armed force shall not be used, save in the common interest, and

to employ international machinery for the promotion of the economic and social advancement of all peoples,

HAVE RESOLVED TO
COMBINE OUR EFFORTS TO
ACCOMPLISH THESE AIMS.

Offering

PEOPLE   We give our money to make this a task force for world order. We give our money to make it possible for others to be a part of the task force in other parts of the world.

Benediction

MINISTER   Go now expecting to be responsible and obedient brothers and sisters in Christ wherever you are, to fulfill God's design in all of life's relationships. And may the peace of God be with you. Amen.

PEOPLE   Amen.

YOUTH SUNDAY

Instrumental Prelude   "Blowin' in the Wind" (*Play through one time, one guitar. All musical line and verse references are for "Blowin' in the Wind."*)

READER   Jesus said to them, "The light is with you for a little longer. Walk while you have the light . . ." (John 12:35).

CHORUS   ". . . for we walk by faith, not by sight" (2 Corinthians 5:7).

READER   "So Jesus came out, wearing the crown of thorns and the purple robe. Pilate said to them, 'Here is the man'" (John 19:05).

VOICE SOLO (*with one guitar; first line, first verse*)

Meditation I   You know how it was when we were younger—pretty easy with someone telling us what to do, where to go, how to act. Now we are facing decisions each day as we are closer to being men and women. When am I a man anyway? At 16 or 17, when I get that coveted driver's license? What about 18? I'm old enough to fight! I can vote at 21 and buy a beer. Some of us have worked at summer and part-time jobs for several years, paying taxes on our income. We have more education than any generation, but less actual responsibility for ourselves and our actions—until we do something wrong. When am I a man?

Instrumental Interlude (*Music rises, fades as reader begins.*)

READER
> "And I say, 'O that I had wings like
>   a dove!
> I would fly away and be at rest . . .'" (Psalm 55:06).

DUET (*with guitars; second line, first verse, sung twice*)

Meditation II   And how far must we go before we rest? "And if any one forces you to go one mile, go with him two miles" (Matthew 5:41). How much is enough? Helping one old lady across the street every day? That tithe given begrudgingly to the church each year? Reluctantly donating to one charity? How much is enough? How far should we go to help another fellow? "But I say to you . . . Love your enemies, bless those who curse you, pray for those who abuse you . . . and you will be sons of the Most High" (Luke 6:27, 35).

Instrumental Interlude   (*Music rises, then fades with reading.*)
READER   "What causes wars, and what causes fightings among you? Is it not your passions that are at war in your members? You desire and do not have; so you kill. And you covet and cannot obtain; so you fight and wage war" (James 4:1, 2).
GROUP SINGING   (*third line, first verse, sung once*)

Meditation III   In April, General Grant began a movement upon Corinth in order to cut the Memphis-Charleston railroad line. On the march his troops were surprised by Confederates under Generals Beauregard and Johnston. A bloody two-day battle ensued at Shiloh.

The fighting in the wilderness region in Virginia was practically continuous from May Fifth to the Twenty-first. Northern casualties were particularly heavy. At Cold Harbor alone, Grant lost over 10,000 men!

On August 6, 1945 occurred an event fraught with immense implications not only for the future of the war, but for the fate of mankind. The bomb was dropped from a B-29 bomber upon the Japanese city of Hiroshima. An area of about 2½ miles in diameter was completely flattened. 129,000 were casualties.

Saigon, South Vietnam, June 23, 1970. Three hundred Reds reported killed in fierce fighting; 69 South Vietnamese. As one American GI expressed, "That's a hell of a waste of human life, no matter who they are!"

GROUP SINGING (*third line, first verse, repeat; then guitars continue to play and fade*)

READER

> "A voice cries:
> 'In the wilderness prepare the way
>   of the LORD,
> make straight in the desert a high-
>   way for our God.
> Every valley shall be lifted up,
>   and every mountain and hill be
>   made low . . .'" (Isaiah 40:3, 4).

CHORUS "Truly, I say to you, whoever says to this mountain, 'Be taken up and cast into the sea,' and does not doubt in his heart, but believes that what he says will come to pass, it will be done for him" (Mark 20:23).

VOICE SOLO (*first line, third verse, sung once; guitars continue, then fade*)

READER

> "Out of my distress I called on the
>   LORD;
> the LORD answered me and set me
>   free" (Psalm 118:05).

CHORUS "For freedom Christ has set us free; stand fast therefore, and do not submit again to a yoke of slavery" (Galatians 5:1).

DUET (*second line, third verse, sung twice*)

Meditation IV You have heard it said that no people ought to be free until they are fit to use their freedom. Have you heard of the fool in the old story who resolved not to go into the water until he had learned to swim? A person can no more learn to swim out of water than he can learn to be a useful part of society outside of that society, or learn to make a choice while someone else makes the choice for him. We are proud that God has given us the opportunity to choose Him or reject Him. Are we more than God that we can make this most important choice or lesser economic and educational choices for another person?

Instrumental Interlude (*music rises, then fades*)

READER   "A man was going down from Jerusalem to Jericho and he fell among robbers, who stripped him and beat him, and departed, leaving him half dead. Now by chance a priest was going down that road; and when he saw him he passed by on the other side. So likewise a Levite, when he came to the place and saw him, passed by on the other side. But a Samaritan, as he journeyed, came to where he was; and when he saw him, he had compassion . . ." (Luke 10:30–33).

GROUP SINGING (*third line, third verse, sung three times and original chorus*)

READER

> "O LORD, our LORD,
> how majestic is thy name in all the
> earth!
> When I look at thy heavens, the
> work of thy fingers,
> the moon and the stars which
> thou hast established;
> what is man that thou art mindful
> of him,
> and the son of man that thou dost
> care for him" (Psalm 8:1, 3, 4)?

VOICE SOLO (*first line, second verse, once*) (*Then instrumental interlude rises and fades.*)

READER

> "O LORD, my God, I call for
> help by day;
> I cry out in the night before thee.
> Let my prayer come before thee,
> incline thy ear to my cry" (Psalm 88:1)!

CHORUS

"He who closes his ear to the cry of
    the poor
will himself cry out and not be
    heard" (Proverbs 21:13).

Meditation V Early one morning in March, 1964, a man attacked a woman as she was returning to her home from work. He stabbed her. She screamed for help and he fled; twice in the next half hour he returned to stab her. She called to her neighbors for help. At least thirty-eight of them heard her, but none of them helped her, and she died. How many times have you read this story and others from across our country since then? I ask, "Who cares?" and the cry comes back from the crowd, "We all care." But where are we when the cry comes for help?

READER "If any man has ears to hear, let him hear" (Mark 4:23).

VOICE DUET (*second line, second verse*)

READER ". . . they stripped him and put a scarlet robe upon him, and plaiting a crown of thorns they put it on his head, and put a reed in his right hand. And kneeling before him, they mocked him saying, 'Hail, King of the Jews!' And they spat upon him, and took the reed and struck him on the head. And when they had mocked him, they stripped him of the robe, and put his own clothes on him and led him away to crucify him" (Matthew 27:28–31).

GROUP SINGING (*third line, second verse is sung three times; then add the following line using the tune of the chorus.*) The answer, my friend, is only in man's faith; the answer is only in his faith.

Folk-Litany Prayer (*sung to "Today"; one voice, one guitar*)

O God, creator of each people and race,
Our witness is here, an unlikely place.
    Reach in our hearts, Thy message make clear,
Strengthen our faith, our belief, in Thy presence here.

We are ready, O God, what first must we do?
Show love and concern—not just to a few.
There isn't much time, and the needs are so great,
Who is my neighbor—how long can I make him wait?

We send out our young men to fight over the sea.
What's wrong with our world, why can't we be free?
O Father, with Your help a new world we'll build,
Then Your wish for our lives will be whole and fulfilled.[2]

LITURGICAL CHOREOGRAPHY

LEADER (*Scripture reading*)

Praise the LORD!
Sing to the LORD a new
song,
his praise in the assembly of the
faithful!
Let Israel be glad in his Maker,
let the sons of Zion rejoice in
their King!
Let them praise his name with
dancing . . . (Psalm 149:1–3).

Praise him for his mighty deeds;
praise him according to his ex-
ceeding greatness!

Praise him with trumpet sound;
praise him with lute and harp!
Praise him with timbrel and dance;
praise him with strings and pipe!
Praise him with sounding cymbals;
praise him with loud clashing
cymbals!

Let everything that breathes praise
the Lord!
Praise the Lord! (Psalm 150:2–6).

Invocation

LEADER   To Thee, O God, we utilize every form and method to
honor Thee, and to express our total affection, submission and
involvement. Grant us minds open to see beauty, to understanding interpretation in movement and rhythm, and to appreciate
our heritage through Jesus Christ. Amen.

Words of Explanation

Liturgical choreography is not contemporary, nor irreligious. For
centuries religious people of the Judaeo-Christian heritage have
used action, bodily movement, and graceful pantomime to
worship God and interpret religious experience. Biblical man
put his whole being into worship: intellect, emotion, volition,
spirit, body—symbolic of total involvement and commitment.
By the use of pantomime and rhythmic movement, they showed
their response to God in fresh, meaningful, personal and
creative ways.

Unlike so many present sanctuary services, Judaic worship was
not something done for them. Every person participated. The
leaders had trumpets; others had flutes, strings, lyres, timbrel
(small drums)—all kinds of instruments. As they entered the
temple in procession, or in the outside sanctuaries (called
dancing meadows), they acted out the mighty acts of God,
such as, the call to Abraham, delivery from Egyptian bondage,
the Passover, entry into Canaan, the time of the judges and
prophets. The interpretive dance is a Biblical and valid worship form.

Nineteen of the Psalms which were used in worship have liturgical "dance" incorporated in them. The purpose was to symbolize the giving of self. When Moses returned from Mount
Sinai, he was angered because the people were dancing to a
golden calf—the wrong object of affection. It had been misused
and prostituted for the wrong "god."

Jesus refers twice to the "dance" (Matthew 11 and Luke 7) using

the reference as a satire to expose the Pharisees. In the cata-
combs, the early Christians danced. Even under persecution,
they praised God. The derivative of Christmas "carol" is a
French word meaning "dance," by which the Incarnation was
interpreted.

So we come today to view the possibilities of beauty and interpretation in liturgical pantomime. In the words of Martha
Graham, "To those who can become as openminded as children,
the dance has a tremendous power; it is a spiritual touch-
stone."

ALL (*congregational hymn*)   "Lord of the Dance"

Interpretive Pantomime and Choreography

PANTOMIME (*during the pantomime Psalms 19 and 121 are read;
this is followed by the singing of "The Lord's Prayer"*)

CONTEMPORARY DANCE   "With A Little Help from My Friends"
by John Lennon and Paul McCartney

BALLET   Rachmaninoff's "Variations on a Theme of Paganini"
from *The Story of Three Loves*—Wanda Pishney

FOLK DANCE   Greek folk dance and "The Hora"

MODERN DANCE TO POETRY   (*While reading "On Beauty" from*
The Prophet *by Kahlil Gibran*)

RELIGIOUS DANCE   "The Creation" from *God's Trombones* by
James Weldon Johnson

Benediction

Postlude   "Countin' My Blessings" from recording of *God's
Trombones.*

CHRISTMAS EVE MIDNIGHT FESTIVAL OF LIGHTS

Scene: Luminarios for exterior lighting are placed outlining church grounds and building. The luminarios are made by using No. 8 paper bags with two inches of damp sand, in which is placed a four-inch candle. These candles will last two hours and produce a gorgeous scene. The youth will place these one yard apart and light them at 10:30 P.M. The entrance and foyer are in dim light with electric lanterns or candles in colored glasses, hung in protected areas.

The following service takes place from 11 P.M. to 12:01 A.M. in the sanctuary which is in diminished light while worshipers gather. The narration, Scripture reading and sound effects can be pretaped, or done live.

NARRATOR   Tonight we have come to celebrate the light that has come into the world. Have you ever been in darkness? (*Lights are gradually extinguished as narrator speaks.*) Complete darkness? . . . Total darkness? . . . All darkness? (*Utter quiet for thirty seconds.*)

In the beginning of time, before creation—"darkness was upon the face of the deep. . . . the earth was without form and void . . ." (*Eerie type music by organ, strings, etc. in minor keys and discord.*)

What confusion, desolation, loneliness, alienation, fear, and desperation there is in darkness. In darkness there are no visible objects, no sense of direction, no beauty, no joy, no meaning. (*Mournful bass chords of organ, lonely tones from flute.*) Then God created light and life. Listen to the description in the Scriptures.

SCRIPTURE READER (*Scripture accompanied by interpretive choreography and appropriate sound effects from harp, flute, drum, timpani and organ*) "In the beginning God created the heavens and the earth. The earth was without form and void, and darkness was upon the face of the deep; and the Spirit of God was moving over the face of the waters. (*Swirl of wire brushes on drum head.*) And God said, 'Let there be light,' and there was light" (Genesis 1:1–31). (*Cymbals and timpani.* PASTOR *or* ACOLYTE *or appointed person enters at this time and lights one large candle at the center of chancel.*)

NARRATOR How good it is to have light! Light illumines the darkness. Light reveals our surroundings. Light brightens the horizon, and makes plants grow, flowers blossom, fruit ripen. Light sustains health and exposes evil. What a blessing to have light, as the Genesis author indicates.

SCRIPTURE READER "And God saw that the light was good; and God separated the light from the darkness. God called the light *Day* (*Crash of cymbal with harp.*) . . . and the darkness he called *Night.* (*Quiet organ.*) And there was evening and there was morning, one day. (*Crash shot on drum, then muffled beat.*) And God said, 'Let there be a firmament in the midst of the waters . . . (*Harp and organ with water effect.*) And let it separate the waters from the waters.' (*Harp.*) And God . . . separated the waters [from] the firmament . . . and God called the firmament Heaven. And there was evening and . . . morning, a second day. (*Crash on drum head, muffled beat resumes.*) And God then created the earth and commanded it to bring forth vegetation and fruit-bearing trees. (*Flute, harp, organ—high ranges.*) And God saw that it was good. And there was evening and there was morning, a third day. (*Crash on drum head, flute.*) And God said, 'Let there be *lights* in the firmament of the heavens to separate the day from the night . . .' (*Light side lights. Flute.*) . . . And God saw that it was good. And there was evening and there was morning, a fourth day. (*Crash on drum head; muffled beat resumes.*) And God said, 'Let the waters bring forth swarms of living creatures, and let birds fly above the earth across the firmament of the heavens.' (*Harp and organ, up and down scale.*) . . . And God blessed them, saying, 'Be fruitful and multiply and fill the waters in the seas and let the birds multiply on the earth.' (*Flute and harp.*) And there was evening and there was morning, a fifth day. (*Crash on drum head, muffled beat resumes.*) And God said, 'Let the earth bring forth living creatures according to their kinds: cattle and creeping things and beasts of the earth according to their kinds.' And it was so. (*Organ with oboe, bassoon stops, etc.*) And God saw that it was good." (*Flute.*)

NARRATOR   Thus, the world was made, light and beautiful, setting the stage for God's supreme creation—man! Listen.

SCRIPTURE READER   "Then God said, 'Let us make man in our image, after our likeness; and let them have dominion over the fish of the sea, and over the birds of the air, and over the cattle, and over all the earth, and over every creeping thing that creeps upon the earth.' (*Clash of cymbals, rim shots on drum, heavy beats on base drum. Loud organ with trumpets, etc.*) So God created man in his own image, in the image of God he created him: male and female he created them. (*Light, beautiful organ and flute.*) And God blessed them and God said to them, 'Be fruitful and multiply, and fill the earth and subdue it; and have dominion over every living thing that moves upon the face of the earth.' (*Organ with trumpet stops, etc.*) . . . And God saw everything that he had made, and behold, it was very good. And there was evening and there was morning, a sixth day." (*Drum heartbeat continues.*)

NARRATOR   This pictures God and all his creatures, including mankind, at peace with one another, living according to the light of God's will. (*Quiet organ, flute and harp.*) However, soon dark, rebellious thoughts entered the mind of man. (*Discord of minor tones from organ.*) Man began to move out on his own, ignoring the light, turning away from God's instruction. This was his sin. (*Timpani.*) Hear how the Bible describes it.

SCRIPTURE READER ". . . men loved darkness rather than light because their deeds were evil. (*Minor tones from organ.*) For everyone who does evil hates the light, and does not come to the light, lest his deeds should be exposed" (John 3:1). (*Organ bass notes.*) (*Choreographers exit.*)

NARRATOR So man became separated from God. Because of this, the world became filled with chaos, war, hate, prejudice, rape, obscenity and death! And the world's light was turned to darkness! (*Flashing on and off of side chancel lights, crash of thunder, crash of drums.*) But God could not bear for man to live in the darkness of sin. So he led Moses to write in words the basis for living meaningfully as human beings with fellow men and God. These Ten Commandments were like lights shining in the darkness.

SCRIPTURE READER (*as two ushers light ten candles at the end of ten pews representing the Commandments. Each may recite one of the Commandments as he does so.*)

You shall have no other gods before me. (*Crash on drum.*)

You shall not make yourself a graven image. (*Crash on drum.*)

You shall not take the name of the Lord your God in vain. (*Crash on drum.*)

Remember the Sabbath Day, to keep it holy. (*Crash on drum.*)

Honor your father and your mother. (*Crash on drum.*)

You shall not kill. (*Crash on drum.*)

You shall not commit adultery. (*Crash on drum.*)

You shall not steal. (*Crash on drum.*)

You shall not bear false witness against your neighbor. (*Crash on drum.*)

You shall not covet . . . (Exodus 20:1–11). (*Crash on drum.*)

NARRATOR   But men love darkness more than light! One by one these lights were ignored and put out! "Give us a golden calf! Give us a king like other nations! Why not steal? Why not kill? What's wrong with adultery? Why not get by with what you can?" Isaiah gives the answer.

SCRIPTURE READER   "Therefore, justice is far from us, (*Organ discord.*) and righteousness does not overtake us; (*Organ discord.*) we look for light, and behold, darkness, (*Lower organ.*) and for brightness, but we walk in gloom. We grope for the wall like the blind, (*Continued lower organ discords.*) we grope like those who have no eyes; (*Organ and slow drum.*) we stumble at noon as in the twilight . . . (59:9–10). (*Organ and slower drum.*) . . . our transgressions are multiplied before thee, and our sins testify against us . . ." (v. 12). (*Lower and lower organ registers throughout this reading.*)

NARRATOR   But God would not leave the world in the condition man's sin had left it. God would not give up in His quest for man's obedience and salvation. He sent His prophets to rekindle the flame of His Kingdom, to give insight to men's minds and to call those in darkness into His marvelous light. (*Cymbals, drums, timpani.*) (*Ushers light one candle at the end of each pew, as prophet's name is recited by each, after which the* NARRATOR *reads from Scripture. A high pitched chime is struck after each.*)

USHER (*lighting first candle*)   Amos.

NARRATOR   ". . . they sell the righteous for silver, and the needy for a pair of shoes—they trample the head of the poor into the dust of the earth, and turn aside the way of the afflicted; . . . my holy name is profaned" (Amos 2:6–7). (*Organ chime.*)

USHER (*lighting second candle*)   Hosea.

NARRATOR   ". . . a spirit of harlotry has led them astray, and they have left their God to play the harlot. . . . a people without understanding shall come to ruin" (Hosea 4:12, 14). (*Organ chime.*)

USHER (*lighting third candle*)   Habakkuk.

NARRATOR   "Behold, he whose soul is not upright in him shall fail, but the righteous shall live by his faith" (Habakkuk 2:4). (*Organ chime.*)

USHER (*lighting fourth candle*)   Ezekiel.

NARRATOR   ". . . as I live, says the Lord God, I have no pleasure in the death of the wicked, but that the wicked turn from his way and live; turn back, turn back from your evil ways . . ." (Ezekiel 33:11). (*Organ chime.*)

USHER (*lighting fifth candle*)   Isaiah.

NARRATOR   "Come now, let us reason together, says the Lord: though your sins are like scarlet they shall be as white as snow; though they are red like crimson, they shall become like wool" (Isaiah 1:18). (*Organ chime.*)

USHER (*lighting sixth candle*)   Micah.

NARRATOR   "He has showed you, O man, what is good; and what does the Lord require of you but to do justice and to love kindness and to walk humbly with your God" (Micah 6:8)? (*Organ chime.*)

USHER (*lighting seventh candle*)   Jeremiah.

NARRATOR   ". . . I will make a new covenant . . . I will put my law within them, and I will write it upon their hearts; and I will be their God, and they shall be my people" (Jeremiah 31:31, 33). (*Organ chime.*)

USHER (*lighting eighth candle*)   Zephaniah.

NARRATOR   "The Lord, your God, is in your midst, . . . he will renew you in his love . . ." (Zephaniah 3:17). (*Organ chime.*)

USHER (*lighting ninth candle*)   Joel.

NARRATOR   ". . . return to me with all your heart, with fasting, with weeping, and with mourning; and rend your hearts and not your garments. Return to the Lord, your God, for he is gracious and merciful, slow to anger, and abounding in steadfast love . . ." (Joel 2:12, 13). (*Organ chime.*)

USHER (*lighting tenth candle*)   Malachi.

NARRATOR   "A son honors his father, and a servant his master. If then I am a father, where is my honor? And if I am a master, where is my fear? Says the Lord of hosts to you" (Malachi 1:6). (*Organ chime.*) Light—yes, plenty of light! But men love darkness more than light, so the words of the prophets were unheeded. (*Organ discord.*) Once again darkness was to fall upon the earth. (*Discordant organ sounds.*)

God had given the word, but it fell upon deaf ears! God had sent the prophets but they were pelted with stones! What could He do now? He must make one final effort. He would send Himself. So He did.

SCRIPTURE READER   "In many and various ways God spoke of old to our fathers by the prophets, but in these last days he has spoken to us by a Son . . . , He reflects the glory of God and bears the very stamp of his nature . . ." (Hebrews 1:1–3).

"In the beginning was the Word, and the Word was with God and the Word was God. (*Drum-like heartbeat.*) He was in the beginning with God; all things were made through him (*Heartbeat.*) and without him was not anything made that was made. In him was life (*Heartbeat.*) and the life was the light of men" (John 1:1–5). (*Flute and harp.*) The true light that enlightens every man was coming into the world (v. 9). And the Word became flesh (*Crash on drum.*) and dwelt among us (*Crash on drum.*) full of grace and truth; (*Flute and harp.*) we have beheld his glory, glory as of the only Son from the Father (v. 14). And from his fulness have we all received, grace upon grace. For the law was given through Moses; grace and truth came through Jesus Christ. No one has ever seen God; the only Son . . . has made him known." (vs. 16–18). (*Beautiful light, happy sounds of organ, flute, harp.*)

NARRATOR   So it came to pass in a little town of Bethlehem, God caused Himself to be born in the flesh. A peasant girl named Mary gave birth to a son whose name was called Jesus. (*Enter choreography interpreters. They perform a dance to "O Holy Night" while an elevated living manger scene is spotlighted. Choreographers interpret song from a lower level than the manger scene.*)

NARRATOR

> O little town of Bethlehem,
>   How still we see thee lie
> Above thy deep and dreamless sleep
>   The silent stars go by.
> Yet in thy dark street shineth
>   The everlasting light
> The hopes and fears of all the years
>   Are met in thee tonight.

SCRIPTURE READER   "The people who walked in darkness have seen a great light; those who dwelt in a land of deep darkness, on them has light shined" (Isaiah 9:2). (*Cymbals, then triumphant sounds from instruments.*)

NARRATOR   But Jesus' ministry, too, was to last only three short years, and the light which God caused to come into the world was to be snuffed out upon a cross of agony and death. (*Lights off manger scene and lights on the cross.*)

SCRIPTURE READER   "He was in the world, and the world was made through him, yet the world knew him not. He came to his own home and his own people received him not" (John 1:10, 11). (*Discordant bass notes of organ, drum.*)

NARRATOR   And once again the world is a jungle of sin with war, hatred, greed, selfishness, riot, rebellion—and darkness hovers over the earth. (*Timpani roll.*) Nevertheless—

SCRIPTURE READER   "The light shines in the darkness and the darkness has not overcome it" (John 1:5). (*Flute.*)

NARRATOR   The world has not overcome that light. God's light in Jesus still shines brightly as the motivation of every noble service, the inspiration for compassion and good will, the illuminator of purpose, the good of brotherhood and peace. (PASTOR *or other person takes a candle and lights it from the central chancel candle.*) There is still hope in our world because of the light that baby brought. The light must be extended to penetrate the darkness. What will you do with the light?

CHOIR (*Anthem*) "Light Just One Little Candle"

USHERS (*come forward to have their candles lit from* PASTOR's *candle, and proceed down aisles to light candles of worshipers in the pews.*)

ALL (*Hymn*) "Joy To The World" (*As candles are lit by worshipers, the* PASTOR *leads them in lifting, lowering and moving candles from side to side as hymn is sung.*)

NARRATOR   Go now into the world with the light you have received. Go, so that love may be known and peace on earth may truly come in the hearts of men.

SCRIPTURE READER   "Let your light so shine before men, that they may see your good works and give glory to your Father who is in heaven" (Matthew 5:16).

CHOIR   *Hallelujah* Chorus

(*Congregation leaves quietly, one row dismissed at a time.*)

MISSIONARY SUNDAY
"Voices of a World in Revolution"

(The following cast appears in this presentation: narrator, quartet of voices, inquisitor.)

NARRATOR

In the first days, God gave man a mind with which
   to think.
Man He also gave a will with which to decide.
With these two man contrived with Greed
And created for himself a force called Power.

From this inclusion dates man's struggle.
From this inclusion dates man's suffering.

So soon as man had the right to power,
So soon did he contrive for himself
The right to suffer:
    To have one man over another
    Is to have one man beneath another;
    It is then, only a matter of time
    Until the equality in which they were both created
    Becomes a part of the forgotten past
    And the present emergency
    Justifies all malefaction.

A powerful few rise to power
While a wise few watch in silent resignation
And a multitude cry from the wilderness that
We
Call
World.

QUARTET
    We are tired of waiting, of hoping;
    We are tired of listening
    To empty promises and foolish lies;
    We no longer want to hear stories
    Of love that breeds greed;
    Of falsehood, hypocrisy and corruption.
    We are tired of hearing
    Voices muffled by power—
    Power which stamps out Truth and Creativity
    And Calls it Love.

    We are tired of hearing promises of peace
    When there is no peace;
    Of help when there is no help,
    Of bread when there is no bread,
    Of life—
        When there is only death and destruction.

FIRST VOICE
      We cry a new theme:
      Give us revolution—
          to erase suppression;

Give us power—
> to make wrong right;

Give us strength—
> to stand for what is good and just.

INQUISITOR

> Yet, my brothers,
> Is it not written
> "Man shall not live by bread alone"?

QUARTET

> This we know:
> Man does live by bread.

INQUISITOR

> Your cries for revolution
> Make you sound like warmongers.
> Has not there been enough blood shed?

FIRST VOICE

> We once sought peace and harmony—
> But men of greed
> And nations of greater greed
> Came to rule our lives
> And steal our minds.
> We too sought wisdom and truth
> But instead we were given dogma and decrees.
> We sought creativity and beauty,
> But instead we were given conformity
> > And production quotas.
> We sought to love those who hated us
> But they killed our children
> And we cannot love those who would
> Destroy us.

SECOND VOICE

> Others promised to help.
> Letters came
> And words gave us hope.

But those who wrote
Wrote from homes safe and secure;
Those who spoke
Spoke of Ideal Lands and Ideal Places
But we live in Reality
With its hate and greed;

We live in Reality;
        Everyday we are hungry;
We live in Reality;
        Everyday we tire from toil.

FIRST AND SECOND VOICES

We hungered and they sent machinery;
We were lonely and they sent money;
We were lost and they used us for their gain;
We were in need and they gave us sermons;
We wanted help and they sent promises.

THIRD AND FOURTH VOICES

Promises!
Promises!
We are tired of promises
Of friends in distant lands
Who send only words;
Of those who use our need
As a means to their power.
We are tired of striving for another's gain;
We are tired of hunger and insecurity.

FIRST AND SECOND VOICES

Give us blood!
Give us revolution!
Give us power!

THIRD VOICE

It is power alone that rules
Power gives us the right to be free
To rule others;

Power gives us strength to
Oppress our oppressors;
Power gives us justice,
For justice, like mercy,
Is the prerogative of the strong.
Give us power and we shall make peace.
We shall slay the oppressor
And set up our own freedom.

INQUISITOR

Power
In your hands would be as bad
As it is in the hands of
Those who hold it now.

NARRATOR

Then what will you give them?

Will you give them new limbs
For shattered bodies?
Will you give them new years
For their ages lost in suppression?
What will you give them
For their youth lost in fighting?
What will you give them
For their dead loved ones?

What will you give them?

INQUISITOR

Why should I give them anything?
What do I owe to them?
I have done nothing wrong
I have done nothing.

FOURTH VOICE

You have done nothing!
Such is your judgment.
You have done nothing wrong,
But you have done nothing.

We are not so
For we must live
With our memories.
We are every day reminded
That our past is still with us.
We cannot forget.

SECOND VOICE

Our people huddled in mud-slung houses
And filth-filled ditches;
Our aching bodies wracked with pain
Yet fighting on for a freedom
Which others inherit by birth;
Our hopeless, mangled mouths gaping for food;
Our dying brothers crying for help;

FIRST VOICE

Our leaders selling our lives
As pawns on a checkerboard globe;
Our councils of war
Bargaining for the lives of countless millions;
Our finest youth, blood of our race,
Brains dashed upon the fruitless rock of greed;

THIRD VOICE

Ghost-faced parents praying in vain
For a son who lies in a cornfield;
Babes crying out for a mother's dried breast;
Stomach-bulging children who stare blankly
Into the face of death,
Knowing it only as life;
Weeping men sobbing blood tears
For a nation lost in
The world's search to become God;

FOURTH VOICE

These we cannot forget.
They ring in our lives,
Resound in our prayers,

Cry out in the night of apathy
And die on the drawing boards of
Dreaming do-gooders.

INQUISITOR

Such words come only from the mouths of fanatics;
Those who have continued to retain the zeal
But who have lost their aim.

We ought to be protected from such nonsense.
There are laws against such people.
Why are not these laws enforced?
What about my rights?
After all, I do know my rights!

NARRATOR

You may know them
But have you earned them?
Do you deserve them?
Do you safeguard them
Or do you let freedom rest on half-attention
And gullible acquiescence
To pretty-mouthed politicians?
You speak of freedom and rights.
How long do you think you shall be free?
How free shall you be while
Man is subject to the power of the mighty?

NARRATOR

No land shall be free until

QUARTET (*in whisper*)

All lands are free.
No power shall last
So long as it is built upon
The weakness of others.
No people shall live for themselves
For they shall perish
Under the might of their own tyranny.

INQUISITOR

You misunderstand me.
I do not like fighting and bloodshed.
Can't we have peace and prosperity too?

QUARTET

But the peace you want this world does not give.
Peace is not the absence of striving.
Peace,
Lost to indifference, self-concern and greed
Must be won with love, reason, and judgment.
The wrong in our lands will not disappear
But rather must be bought
With innocent blood
By a higher law of love.

SECOND VOICE

Not until men see in man the fear of pain;
Not until man has learned
To care for his brothers
To the farthest reach of the world;
Not until love is more important than self;

QUARTET

Then shall the world find peace.
The peace which passes
Beyond our understanding.

NARRATOR

Great, great is the need for love,
As great as the need for peace.[3]

Amen.

CELEBRATING THE COMING OF AGE

(*An occasion when sons and daughters become thirteen years old. The participants include the minister, two boys, two girls, community of parents and young people.*)

Statement of Intention (*Word of welcome from the minister to the new teen-agers and why the church considers this threshold of life an occasion for joy and celebration.*)

The Common Meal (*Cheeseburgers for everyone with milk shakes for honorees and coffee for their parents. Table decorations: figures from Peanuts cartoons with Peanuts napkins and a big Snoopy lying on his doghouse providing the centerpiece.*)

Peanuts Cartoons and Discussion (*After viewing a series of Peanuts slides, the new teen-agers discuss the several traits and problems represented.*)

The Prayers of Confession (*Prayers by young people following discussion*)

ALL   Almighty God, Father of our Lord Jesus and Judge of us all; we are sorry for our sins.

FIRST GIRL   Like Lucy, we look for a scapegoat. We demand that the world be perfect. We are determined to walk over people before they walk over us. We want life to be *yes, yes, yes* with never a *no.*

FIRST BOY   Like Charlie Brown, we've been confused from the day we were born. We feel out of place on the earth. We feel unloved. The goat in us rises instead of the hero. We're wishy-washy.

SECOND GIRL   Like Snoopy, we make great plans and put them off until after supper. We try to be something we aren't, as he pretends to be a wolf, a vulture, or a penguin.

SECOND BOY   Like Linus, no problem is so big or so complicated that it can't be run away from. We expect nothing as a gift, but feel it has to be earned. We need a blanket. We can't face life unarmed. We sit in the pumpkin patch waiting for the wrong saviour. The whole trouble with us is—we won't listen to what the whole trouble with us is.

The Word to the Parents

To be a parent in your children's teen-age years is to be

—anxious as to whether or not you have responsibly prepared your children to live in the freedom and maturity of the Word in Jesus Christ.

—threatened by their new need to find fault with you as an adult.

—surprised that some of their interests and concerns are altogether different from what you have projected for them; proving that they are distinctly "other" and not an extension of yourself.

—confused by their resentment when treated as a child; and yet their reaching out in subtle ways to continue in a dependent role, which always makes the parent wonder just what they want and what they need.

The Word to the New Teen-agers

To be a person in your teen-age years is to be

—discovering that your parents are fallible, with faults and insecurities of their own; which is both a frightening and a relieving discovery to make.

—changing so rapidly that you are faced with a new self you hardly know; a body so uneven in its growth that it sometimes makes you clumsy; your friends of different sizes; and your sexual awareness as a strange and wonderful new gift.

—confused about your own behavior which but a few years ago was acceptable unto your parents, but which suddenly seems immature to them in light of a new adult behavior they now expect, and in which you've had no experience.

—hesitant in seeking out advice even when you know you need it.

—critical for the first time in your life of how your mother scrambles eggs or how your father drives a car.

The Word to Both Young People and Parents

These common but perplexing experiences that parents and their children share are but the signs and symbols of an emergent and authentic life. Little birds are pushed from nests, ducklings are taught to swim, and human mothers undergo the anguish of a second giving birth as each child cuts the cord and begins to move toward his own maturity and selfhood. Fathers are in pain at having to decide at times to let their children experiment by trial and error when all along "he could have told them how the experiment comes out." And young people are in innumerable despairs over having to hurt the ones they love the most; first by breaking from them, then needing them again; going it alone, then returning to the fold. There is no other way to life, except through fits and starts; and we have no guarantee along the way of whether each of us has acted wisely or what the final outcome is going to be. All we know is that this is the tempo of creation, the great reality of birthing through which the Creator God calls each person into being. So that what now appears to us as risk and threat may be also seen as the sacramental gift called life.

The Litany of the Coming of Age

COMMUNITY   O Lord, our heavenly Father, we, Thy humble servants, desire Thy fatherly goodness mercifully to accept this our sacrifice of praise and thanksgiving.

YOUNG PEOPLE   We commit to Thee our desire to make choices on our own, and our fear that we will be left alone if we choose wrongly.

PARENTS We praise Thee for our children's drive to risk right and wrong choices, and acknowledge our reluctance to let them make their own mistakes.

YOUNG PEOPLE We commit to Thee our need to have someone listen to us and understand.

PARENTS We praise Thee for our children's struggle to be heard, and acknowledge our frequent failure to hear what they are saying.

YOUNG PEOPLE We commit to Thee the strangeness of our new and changing bodies, their mystery and wonder as we come of age as men and women.

PARENTS We praise Thee for this season of our children's physical maturity, and acknowledge our uncertainty about how far to trust them with this new gift.

YOUNG PEOPLE We commit to Thee the new importance of our friends outside the family, and the gradual possibility of being less dependent on our parents.

PARENTS We praise Thee for our children's new relationships, and acknowledge our desire to see their friends and heroes enhance their true maturity and independence.

YOUNG PEOPLE We commit to Thee the new questions we are beginning to ask about our faith.

PARENTS We praise Thee for the traditions of our community, and acknowledge our children's need to risk the kind of questions that will make a firsthand faith a lively option in their seeking.

COMMUNITY Through Jesus Christ our Lord, by whom and with whom, in the unity of the Holy Spirit, all honor and glory be unto Thee, O Father Almighty, world without end. Amen.

MINISTER I send you forth as families, struggling with freedom and responsibility, dependence and independence, security and risk; and pronouncing all of this as good in the providence and love of the eternal God.[4]

COMMUNITY Amen.

A WORSHIP COLLAGE
FOR YOUTH CONFERENCE [5]

MUSIC *"The Voyage"* (*On tape or record.*)

READER (*Collect*) We are a part of what we see. What we
see and do is what we become. Choose what you see and you
choose in great part who you are. Have imagination. Dream.
Have new thoughts. Take a world. See it. Call it by name.
Show it to another. Tell it to God. Lay it on the altar. Break it
like bread. It is your world. Bless it!

SOLOIST "There's A World Out There"

ALL (*Confession*) We confess that we are accomplices with the
demonic powers of violence.

We live richly on oppression.

We sleep in beds of prejudice; we speak well of love and
curse our enemy.

We take pride in freedom and invent new slavery.

We say that our goal is peace and prepare instruments of
war.

We cry out against exploitation and we exploit each other.

So we are accomplices in the crime of starving bodies, despairing ghettoes, abused freedom.

We are accomplices by turning our faces away and of doing
nothing.

READER (*Lesson from the Old Testament*) Job 32:6–10 (the RSV
translation)

ALL (*Song*) "Earth Song" by Donald D. Chen (*the words are
included here, but the music is to be created by the participating group*)

Slipping past Jupiter, flying past Mars
Stepping on the Moon, I'm half way to the stars
But when I turned around, guess what I did see?
The whole earth waving, saying "hello" to me.

Chorus

It's the whole earth, it's the whole earth
It's the whole earth, oh yes indeed.
It's the whole earth, it's the whole earth
It's the whole earth, for you and me.

Well I've been to Jupiter, and it's real cold
And that Mars ain't got life, it's very old
Been to the Moon, it's full of that dust
So now I'm coming home, cause you know that I must.

Repeat Chorus

Now it's quite a view, from way out in space,
This death of ours don't look so big, I can't see your face
Now tell me babe, where can you go hide?
So it's you and me, we're on the same side.

Repeat Chorus

So I'll travel on in this world, spreading the Word
Stop all I meet on the road, to tell them the Word.
To all good people for all that it's worth
We're born, we're born, on this whole earth.

Repeat Chorus

We are the people, we are the people
We are the people, we are the people
Of the whole earth.

Sermon: Mass on the Word (*five readers participate*)

FIRST READER   In the beginning was Power, intelligent, loving, energizing.

SECOND READER   In the beginning was the Word, supremely capable of mastering and molding whatever might come into being in the world of matter.

THIRD READER   In the beginning were not coldness and darkness; there was Fire.

FOURTH READER   This is the truth.

FIFTH READER   In the new humanity which is begotten today the Word prolongs the unending act of his own birth;

FIRST   And by virtue of his immersion in the world's womb the great waters of the kingdom of matter have, without even a ripple, been endued with life.

SECOND   Through our thoughts and human experiences, we long ago became aware of the strange properties which make the universe so like our flesh.

THIRD   Like the flesh it attracts us by the charm which lies in the mystery of its curves and folds and in the depth of its eyes;

FOURTH   Like the flesh it disintegrates and eludes us when submitted to our analyses.

FIFTH   As with the flesh, it can only be embraced in the endless reaching out to attain what lies beyond the confines of what has been given us.

FIRST   Shatter, my God, through the daring of your revelation the childishly timid outlook that can conceive of nothing greater or more vital in the world than the pitiable perfection of our own human organism.[6]

Interpretive Choreography   "Exploration of Space" (*This consists of three parts, improvised by the liturgical dance interpreters; one, individual space; two, dual space; three, group space. As suggested, the sections are performed individually, in couples, then en masse. Creative selections of music and lyrics can make this a most meaningful experience.*)

Dialogue Discussion   "The Party" (*Here a tape collage is played including discussion of drugs, politics, war, peace, and religion as might be done informally at a young people's gathering. Interspersed music might include "Blowin' In The Wind" by Bob Dylan, "The Great Mandella" from Album 1700 by Peter, Paul* *and Mary, "Superstar—John Nineteen Forty-one" by Murray Head.)*

The Agape Common Meal (*The five readers take some home-made bread and several goblets of wine, and pass through the informally gathered congregation giving them the "spiritual food." While distributing the emblems, a soloist with guitar sings and leads congregation in singing "Bread Of Life."*)

Intercession Prayer (*responsive*)

LEADER   When a mind is closed and communication has ceased, how may a person be reached? If his heart has never learned to love, or has stopped loving, how may the heart be taught, Jesus?

RESPONSE   We have come together to be served by God's word. Let us examine ourselves honestly and stand before the Word as we really are.

LEADER   We are afraid to involve ourselves deeply in Life. We shirk the responsibility we have for others and ourselves. We pretend to care but really live in selfishness.

RESPONSE   Lord, have mercy upon us.

LEADER   The word is not the Word until it is enacted.

RESPONSE   We, having heard the Word, decide to live in action.

LEADER   Life is our mission.

RESPONSE   We choose to be sent.

LEADER   Let us send ourselves.

RESPONSE   We invest our love and lives together with those of our brothers.

LEADER   Let us be one.

RESPONSE   All lives are one in the Lord.

LEADER   In the whole earth.

RESPONSE   Amen.[7]

Offering (*The five readers go through the congregation to receive the offering gifts. The soloist leads the congregation in singing "Pass It On."*)

Benediction

> Time is hunger, space is cold
> Pray, pray for prayer alone can quiet
> The anxieties of the void.
>
> Dream is a solitary rock
> Where the soul's hawk nests:
> Dream, dream, during
> Ordinary life.

SOLOIST (*song*)   "Taps" (*Sung softly and reflectively.*)

Passing of the Peace (*a hug and holy kiss is passed from person to person*)

LEADER   Go now in peace.

YOUTH COFFEEHOUSE SERVICE
"The Caring Crowd"

Beginning (*Informally the youth gather around small tables, or on the floor. They sing many folk ballads and mood songs accompanied by guitars or ukuleles, ending with a quiet one with words conducive to worship.*)

Silent Prayer (*The* LEADER *then asks each youth to say a silent prayer for each one at his particular table or group.*)

Scripture Interpretation (*The* LEADER *then asks each group to think about his interpretation of Matthew 18:30, "Where two or three are gathered together in my name, there am I in the midst of them." One or two groups read their interpretation. The* LEADER *then explains that they are gathered as the "Koinonia"*) in Christ, the caring crowd. Christ cared for others, so the Koinonia is a "caring community.")

(Each group is then given a sheet of paper containing a particular Scripture related to caring for others out of Christian love, such as, Galatians 6:2, "Bear you one another's burdens and so fulfil the law of Christ"; or, John 13:34, "A new commandment I give to you, that you love one another . . ."; or 1 John 4:7, 8, ". . . for love is of God, and he who loves is born of God and knows God. He who does not love does not know God, for God is love.")

(Each group then takes the sheet and writes in poem form about the lesson. Each person writes one or two lines, and passes it on, until everyone in the group has contributed to the poem. Each group takes the microphone and shares their contribution, the LEADER acting as monitor.)

The Act of Love (All the groups put their tables together, so all can sit in a large circle. The LEADER—or host—places pretzels in moderate piles around the oblong table. Each youth takes one.)

LEADER   Some of you have already begun to eat your own pretzel. This demonstrates that we really think of ourselves first, and that we give lip service to loving our brother. If we were really serious about being the "Caring Crowd," we would share, and see that our neighbor was fed first. If you now will take your pretzel—or get another—and feed it to your partner—or neighbor—saying these words, "Because Christ Cared I Care." (Each youth then feeds another. When finished, the LEADER takes a can of soft drink.)   You will be given a drink. It symbolizes that you are all thirsty for another's caring. Share yours with the person on either side of you.

THE ONE TO BE GIVEN DRINK   I thirst.

THE ONE SERVING   Because Christ gave living water with his love, take this and my love.

Closing (The Lord's Prayer is prayed in unison as the benediction.)

YOUTH SENSITIVITY GROUP
"The Sightless Made to See"

Beginning (*young people gather in a circle, seated on either chairs or the floor*)
READER   John 9:13–41.

Introduction of Blind Guest
LEADER   What does it mean to be blind? How does a person feel? Have you ever known or met a blind person? (*Introduces guest who has been invited to come because he or she is blind and asks guest to tell what it is like to be blind. How does he feel? What are his problems? How does he adjust? What changes are experienced? How does he "see" without sight?*)

Identification and Sensitivity Practice (*Each young person is asked to close his eyes, then walk to another person and learn as much as possible by feeling the hands of his neighbor. He continues with eyes closed, feeling the faces of others in an effort to learn something meaningful through touching and listening that will provide identification and a new and deeper appreciation of the others. Five minutes should be devoted to this experience.*)

Sharing (*paper bags are distributed to be used over the heads so none can see*)
LEADER (*inviting replies from volunteers*)   Is it possible to "have eyes but see not?" What does it mean "to be made to see?"
LEADER (*passing "the peace" with folded hands into the hands of the person next to him*)   May the sight of Christ be yours. (*Person removes bag from head and passes peace to his neighbor until all have received "the sight of Christ."*)

A WEDDING CEREMONY

MINISTER   Marriage is as old as the human family. It is the highest of life's relationships. It is of the ordaining of the Creator
in the very nature of our being as man and as woman. God's
fatherly intention toward his children is revealed through this
relationship.

The occasion that declares publicly the intention of a man
and a woman to enter into this relationship has become known
in our society as a wedding. For the Christian, this occasion
is not spectacle, but worship; it is not a mere formal observance, but a participation in the will of God for life. A wedding
is the celebration of the highest we know in love—the pledging
of the deepest fidelity—the expression of the highest aspiration.
A relationship so sacred must not be entered into casually or
flippantly but thoughtfully and deliberately.

On this occasion _____ and _____ come
before family, friends, and church to affirm the choice that they
have made of each other as a life's mate and their intention
to establish a home for the raising of a family and the fulfilment of life together.

_____ and _____, as you contemplate
the making of your vows to each other, realize that henceforth
your destinies shall be woven of one design and your perils
and your joys shall not be known apart. The words, "I love
you," first spoken shyly in months gone by, when it was not
known if they would be accepted or returned in kind, are
today spoken in the full commitment of yourselves to each
other and to an adult responsibility in society.

How like the church in its relationship to its Lord is the wedding of two of God's children! May you see in the relationship of Christ and His church the pattern of love and devotion you will need to have toward one another that the church may truly be "in your house." The resourcefulness of Christian love for this, and for all of life's relationships, has been declared by the Apostle Paul in his unforgettable words: "Love seeks not its own. It is patient and understanding and is not easily provoked. Love does not gloat over the faults of the other, but affirms his or her good. Love is not judgmental, but forgives. It believes all things." Love never ends. This many-splendored love must be the substance of the vows that you make to each other; for "except the Lord build the house, they labor in vain who build it." (*Paraphrased from 1 Corinthians 13*)

Let us pray: Out of this tangled world, O God, You have drawn together these two persons and are binding them firmly by the sure insights of love. We thank You for the homes in which _____ and _____ have been nurtured in the formative years of their lives; for parents who have sacrificed in their behalf and made possible opportunities of education; for the church which has awakened them to the meaning of eternal life.

Our Father, bless these as they come before family, friends, and church to affirm the choice that they have made of each other as a life's mate and their intention to establish a home where Your love may be celebrated in the family. Grant them a seriousness of purpose that they may be delivered from empty words and casual commitments. For the fulfilment of their vows, may they discern the varied facets of Your many-splendored love. May Your Word nurture them all the days of their lives that their dreams and aspirations for life may find fulfilment in the doing of Your will in all things.. As we share with them in the celebration of love on this occasion, may we all grow toward the perfection that is experienced in Your love. Through Him who so hallowed the wedding feast in Cana with His presence that the guests experienced a joy that they had never known before, we pray. Amen.

MINISTER (*to the* GROOM) Are you, _____, ready to enter this holy relationship, to accept the responsibilities of a husband; to be _____'s loving, faithful, and helpful husband whether in days of success or adversity? (*The* GROOM *answers: "I am."*)

MINISTER (*to the* BRIDE) Are you, _____, ready to enter this holy relationship, to accept the responsibilities of a wife; to be _____'s loving, faithful, and helpful wife whether in days of success or adversity? (*The* BRIDE *answers: "I am."*)

By these answers, which you have given after due consideration and serious thought, your purpose and willingness to take one another for better or for worse from this day forward is affirmed.

MINISTER Who gives _____ to be married to _____? (*The* BRIDE'S FATHER *answers: "Her mother and I do."*)

As a further indication of your readiness to enter into this relationship, will you join your right hands, and repeat individually after me the marriage vows.

MINISTER (*to the* GROOM) "I, _____, take you, _____ to be my wife, to have and to hold—from this day forward—for better or for worse—to love—to cherish—and to honor—till death do us part."

MINISTER (*to the* BRIDE) "I, _____, take you, _____, to be my husband; to have and to hold—from this day forward—for better or for worse—to love—to cherish—and to honor—till death do us part."

MINISTER (*continues*) Are there rings to further seal these vows? From the earliest time, the golden circle has been a symbol of wedded love. It is made of pure gold to symbolize pure love. Being one unbroken circle, it symbolizes unending love. As often as either of you see these golden circles, you will be reminded of this high moment and the unending love you promise.

MINISTER (*to the* GROOM)   Take this ring and place it upon the wedding finger of _____ _____ and repeat: "With this ring I thee wed; in the name of the Father, and of the Son, and of the Holy Spirit." Amen.

MINISTER (*to the* BRIDE)   Take this ring and place it upon the wedding finger of _____ and repeat: "This ring I give thee, in token and pledge of our constant faith and abiding love." (*Wording may be revised for single ring ceremony.*)

Since you have promised your love to each other, and before God and these witnesses have exchanged these solemn vows, and these symbols of genuine and undying love, as a minister of the Gospel of Jesus Christ, I pronounce you husband and wife. "What therefore God has joined together, let no man put asunder" (Matthew 19:6).

MINISTER   Let us kneel for Communion.[8]

In the ancient oriental world a personal covenant of loyalty was practiced by simply partaking of bread and drink.

To break faith with one with whom one had broken bread was a most heinous sin. When loved ones were to be separated, they broke bread and drank a toast together as a pledge of love and loyalty, even at the sacrifice of body and blood.

Take eat . . . drink. . . . This is the seal of your covenant. Let us unite in praying the Lord's Prayer.

Now may God's joy which the world cannot give and which the world cannot take away be yours today and tomorrow and in all of life's tomorrows. Amen.

(*Couple seals covenant with kiss.*)

WEDDING WORSHIP SERVICE

Prelude Recital:
"Rejoice Greatly, O my Soul"—S. Karg-Elert
"Jesu, Joy of Man's Desiring"—Bach
"From God I Ne'er Will Turn Me"—D. Buxtehude
"Suite Gothique"—L. Boellmann
"O Perfect Love"—Barnby

OPENING HYMN   "Love Divine"—Zundel (*Mothers are escorted during the singing, congregation standing.*)

Call to Worship   We are met here to present _____ and _____ before God to be united in marriage, in accord with the agelong truth, verified by experience, "It is not good that man should be alone (Genesis 2:18), . . . therefore, a man leaves his father and his mother, and shall cleave unto his wife; and they become one flesh (Genesis 2:24)."

Invocation Prayer   O God, who alone unites persons in holy bonds of covenant, without whose Spirit there is no abiding unity: be present in the inner being of these who desire to be married, and among these whose sacred responsibility it is to give or withhold approval—in the Spirit of Christ, the Lord, Amen.

PROCESSIONAL   "Trumpet Voluntary in D"—Purcell (*Wedding party proceeds to bottom of chancel steps.*)

The Meditation Concerning Marriage   Of all the human events, none more easily becomes an occasion for rejoicing than does marriage. Even the dullest person alive can hardly fail to have a sense of wonder as he sees a man and woman take their places before an altar and pledge their lifelong devotion to each other.

Science and art are efforts to find unity in diversity . . . but marriage not only discovers unity, but undertakes to create unity. Two lives, belonging to different sexes, and often with widely different biological backgrounds, come together in the sight of God and before their friends to inaugurate something never seen in the world before—their particular combination of inheritance and their particular union of personalities. They join their destinies in such a manner that sorrow for one will be sorrow for the other and good fortune for one will be good fortune for the other. Marriage has a mystical quality because it combines the flesh and spirit in remarkable unity, the closest physical intimacy that is possible. Moreover, the normal expected result of their union will be the coming into the world of new persons, who, apart from this union, would never have been granted the possibility of existence.

Marriage, then, is a sharing in the entire creative process and a window through which the meaning of human existence shines with unusual brilliance.[9]

The Charge to the Congregation   True marriage can never be private or secret, because it has a public character. Not only on their wedding day, but in its entire course, it is a public affair. The community has a stake in this creative union and its offspring, and deserves the joy of participation. The community and families involved come today to give symbolic approval and blessing to your union. What happens at the altar is the stamp of approval of the Christian community. The miracle happens, not at the altar, but when you two people realize that the fulness of life for you involves a complete unity of destiny. This religious ceremony is designed so that you may make vows of lifelong fidelity, in the presence of those whose approbation and blessing you seek.

The Symbolic Approval   Now who will, in behalf of the families and their beloved community, give the stamp of approval for this woman _____ to become the wife of this man _____

FATHER OF THE BRIDE   I do.

The Declaration of Intention (*Traditionally, this was performed on the church steps at the time of the engagement announcement. Later it was incorporated into the actual wedding service. To allow the* BRIDE *and* GROOM *to go together to the altar, this should be done at the bottom of the chancel steps.*)   Marriage is fraught with tremendous possibility of failure and success as well as pain and joy. The possibility of sorrow and of happiness is greater in married life than in single life. The person who has not made the wager of devotion cannot be hurt by the unfaithfulness of another as can the person who makes the leap of faith, nor can he know the sublimity of the joyous, majestic heights as the one who shares in depth with a trusted, compatible companion.

Are you ready in the presence of this community to declare your intention to make this venture of faith and love?

_____ are you willing to receive _____ as your wife, having full confidence that your abiding faith in each other as human beings will last a lifetime? *Answer:* I am.

_____ are you willing to receive _____ as your husband, having full confidence that your abiding faith in each other as human beings will last a lifetime? *Answer:* I am.

PASTOR'S PRAYER   Heavenly Father, who ordained marriage for your children, and endowed us with creative ability in love, we present to Thee these who have disclosed their wish to be married. May their union be endowed with true devotion, spiritual commitment, and personal integrity. O God, give to this woman, _____, and to this man _____, the ability to keep the covenant between them made. When selfishness shows itself, grant generosity; when mistrust is a temptation, give moral strength; where misunderstanding intrudes, give patience and gentleness. When suffering becomes their lot, give them a strong faith and abiding hope.

If You should bless their home with children, give them the qualities of true and wise parenthood. Make their home a shelter from that which corrupts and destroys, and may it be a school wherein they may be fitted for Thy Kingdom. Amen.

SOLOIST "Love Never Faileth"—Root *or* "Love Is Kind and Suffers Long"—Capetown (*Couple moves to prie-dieu*)

The Exchange of Wedding Vows Marriage requires much of generosity, unselfishness, flexibility, Christian forbearance and grace from both husband and wife. Under it lies the sober responsibility of home and community, but when it is supported by all the strength and commitments of love and charity, those burdens are delightful. Marriage is the mother of the world, and the nursery of heaven, filling cities and churches with the Kingdom of Christ. The reality and happiness of your marriage depends upon the inner experience of your heart and the integrity of your commitment.

As a seal of your covenant, you [each] have chosen ring(s) of precious metal, symbolizing the unity, wholeness and endlessness of your life together. (MINISTER *takes rings; to* GROOM) Will you place this ring upon the wedding finger of your bride, and say your promise to her?

GROOM (*giving memorized vows*) In the presence of the Lord and before these friends, I, _____Carl [Jean, take you, Jean [Car_____, to be my wife, promising with Christ's Spirit, to be your loving and faithful husband, in prosperity and in need, in joy and in sorrow, in sickness and in health, to honor and cherish you, and respect your privileges as an individual as long as we both shall live. As this ring has no end, neither shall my love for you.

(To BRIDE, if a double ring ceremony) Will you place this ring upon the wedding finger of your groom and say your promise to him? [see p. 74] [Or, if single ring ceremony, "As you receive this ring, say your promise to him."]

BRIDE (*giving memorized vows*) In the presence of the Lord and before these friends, I, ___Jean___, take you ___Car___ ___, to be my husband, promising with Christ's Spirit, to be your loving and faithful wife, in prosperity and in need, in joy and in sorrow, in sickness and in health, to honor and cherish you, and give encouragement as long as we both shall live. As this ring has no end, neither shall my love for you. Wherever you go, I will follow; where you live, I will live; your people shall be my people, and your God my God for as long as we both shall live.

The Charge to the Couple (*couple kneeling*) If marriage is to be maintained at a high level of mutual benefit, the sacred aspect must be continued throughout its entire course. Two people are not married in the ceremony of an hour; you only begin to be married. What is begun must continue with growing meaning as long as life shall last.

The dangers which married life faces are so great that only a strong moral commitment and spiritual motivations can last. Mere physical attractiveness will not suffice. Only the love of God will suffice.

The Lord's Prayer (*in unison*)

Our Father, who art in heaven, Hallowed be Thy name. Thy Kingdom come, Thy will be done, on earth as it is in heaven. Give us this day our daily bread. And forgive us our sins, as we forgive those who sin against us. And lead us not into temptation, but deliver us from evil. For thine is the Kingdom and the power and the glory, forever. Amen.

The Declaration of Marriage (*couple stands*)   Since you _____ and _____ have consented together to be married, and have witnessed the same before God and this community of relatives and friends, and have committed love to and faith in each other, and have sealed the promises with rings, I announce that God has made you husband and wife.

The Communion Greater love has no one than this—that he sacrifice himself, and lay down his life for the other, as did our Lord. So may we partake of His Spirit as we consume the elements of His love. (*Couple eats the bread and the cup is served to them.*) Let us pray:

Benediction Now, may the courage of the early morning's dawning, and the strength of the eternal hills, and the peace of the evening's ending, and the love of God be in your hearts now and evermore. Amen.

MODERN FUNERAL SERVICE

PRELUDE MUSIC

INTRODUCTORY SENTENCES Someone very dear to all of us here has died. We are saddened because the separation seems so final. We recount now the years of joy, the associations in laughter, work, family and service.

> Bless the Lord, O my soul,
> and forget not all his benefits . . . (Psalm 103:2).

AFFIRMATION OF FAITH Our faith is affirmed in the words of Jesus: "I am the living bread which came down from heaven; if anyone eats of this bread he will live for ever . . ." (John 6:51). ". . . I am the resurrection and the life; he who believes in me, though he die, yet shall he live . . ." (John 11:25). ". . . I am the way and the truth and the life; no one comes to the Father but by me. If you had known me, you would have known my Father also . . ." (John 14:6).

And Paul boldly affirmed, "If it is for this life only that Christ has given us hope, we of all men are most to be pitied" (1 Cor. 15:19 NEB). "As in Adam all die, so also in Christ shall all be made alive" (1 Cor. 15:22).

INVOCATION Father God, Your infinite love was made manifest in the cross, and Your infinite power was demonstrated in the resurrection; grant Your holy comfort to abide with these, our dear bereaved friends, until the day is over. May Your promise find fulfilment for our departed one, through Jesus Christ, who taught us to pray:

UNISON (The Lord's Prayer): Our Father in heaven; holy be your name. Your Kingdom come, your will be done, on earth as in heaven. Give us today our daily bread. Forgive us our sins, as we forgive those who sin against us. Save us from the time of trial, and deliver us from evil. For yours is the Kingdom, the power and the glory forever. Amen.

MEDITATION Death is not what we have thought it to be. It is the step from transient to permanent, from temporary to eternal.

From the caterpillar emerges the butterfly;

From the grain blossoms the full blown sheath,

From the child, the adolescent is born. So in death, the years of training are over, so that the eternal work may start. The last rehearsal is finished so that the play may begin. One class of school is graduated so that another degree may commence.

Oh death—grotesque character, horror of children, foe of the fearful—take off your mask! You terrify the world. You frighten and deceive men. You bring sorrow with separation. Your sting is great.

Yet, your reason for happening is to open the door of escape from one room to give entrance to another. You are not able to take from us those that we love.

But where are they, those that we have loved? Are they in

ecstasy, taken up in holy fellowship? Are they tormented in the night, burning with frustration and anxiety? Are they in lonely despair, because they loved not God?

Not at all! With what they left this life, they begin the new existence. Our eyes cannot see them because they have left their bodies for a time, as one steps out of his clothing.

However, in the Lord, we never lose our own. We know they live eternally in the spirit eternal. They are vividly present in the presence of love. We meet them when we meet the Lord. We receive them when we receive the Lord. O loved ones, eternally alive, help us to learn in this short life how to live eternally through the quality of love.

BENEDICTION   Now let faith and hope abide because we have drunk deeply of your love, O God.

POSTLUDE   "I Have Found Your Love In This Place"

ADDITIONAL MEDITATION

Friends, God alone understands the sense of loss which you here have sustained in the death of _____. So let us pray to Him. O God, whom we do not know as we would like, yet whom we acknowledge as the source of all life and the sustainer beyond death; we do not ask for escape from our grief and sorrow. We only pray for a renewed faith in the reality of the unseen, and the promises of Jesus who brought life, hope and immortality to light. Amen.

I do not want you to think of this so much as a "funeral service" but as a memorial and tribute to _____. We recall with tender appreciation our personal associations with him (or her). Each of us will recall different details of laughter, work, school, family, recreation, conversations, experiences and services for which we are especially thankful.

May you who feel this loss most profoundly, find comfort, meaning and hope in these testimonies from sacred Scripture: "The Lord is my Shepherd, I shall not want . . . Even though I walk through the valley of the shadow of death, I fear no evil; for thou art with me; thy rod and thy staff, they comfort me" (Psalm 23:1, 4). "Let not your hearts be troubled; believe in God, believe also in me. In my Father's house are many rooms; if it were not so, would I have told you that I go to prepare a place for you? And when I go and prepare a place for you, I will come again and will take you to myself, that where I am you may be also" (John 14:1–3). ". . . and death shall be no more, neither shall there be mourning nor crying nor pain any more, for the former things have passed away" (Revelation 21:4).

Let us pray: O Father of Mercy, we tenderly thank You for this life we have loved so much. Forgive our sins of omission and commission. Relieve our feelings of remorse. We commend _____ to Thy keeping, believing in Thy eternal love and the power of resurrection through Jesus Christ. O Blessed Hope! O Blessed Peace! All is well through Jesus Christ. Amen.

We are never more a community in Christ than in these moments, for we dare to gather in the face of death and proclaim the word, dry weeping eyes, declare our mutual dependence and celebrate.

In the large perspective, we do gather here for celebration. Not celebration that death has come, but that God is God, the Father and sustainer of the Jesus-like life and spirit. Our celebration is not centered in some guarantee or specific prediction of what happens to us after death. We simply give ourselves and our dead into the hands of One whose love is the only certainty that lies beyond our fragile forecast. We know that in death as in life we are in Him, and that is enough to know. "We know that in everything God works for good with those who love him, who are called according to his purpose" (Romans 8:28).

We go forth to continue living in the certainty that life and death are gracious gifts from God who fills both of them with meaning.

"Let us then with confidence draw near to the throne of grace, that we may receive mercy and find grace to help in time of need" (Hebrews 4:16). "It is the LORD who goes before you; he will be with you, he will not fail you or forsake you; do not fear or be dismayed" (Deuteronomy 31:8). "He only is my rock and my salvation . . ." (Psalm 62:2).

O God—a very precious person has left our midst. We are glad for the glow of faith and hope that rises in our hearts through the knowledge of Jesus Christ, who verified that love is stronger than hate, that life outlasts death, and who assured us, saying, ". . . because I live, you will live also" (John 14:19). Glory be to Thee. Amen.

Section 2

DEVOTION GUIDES

Christian Calendar

Paraphrased Scriptures

Modern Parables

Prayers

Meditations

THE CHRISTIAN CALENDAR

The Christian Year is the church's way of following God's revelation in the life of Jesus Christ. As the seasons unfold, beginning with Advent, the pattern of Christ's life appears, giving Christians insight into the Word of God, and an opportunity to respond meaningfully.

Pre-Christmas or Advent A four-week period in which the church joyfully remembers the coming of Christ, and prepares for another celebration. Beginning with the Sunday nearest November 30, the season is observed for the four Sundays prior to Christmas.

> Season of penitence, preparation and anticipation of Christ's birth.
>
> Color: purple for penitence
>
> Symbols: Advent wreath of four candles, lighting one candle each of the four Sundays.

Christmas and Post-Christmas or Christmastide Begins Christmas Day, December 25, and continues for twelve days.

> Season of Incarnation, celebrating the birth of Jesus.
>
> Color: white for joy and purity
>
> Symbols: *Chi Rho.* First two letters XP of the word "Christ" in ancient Greek capital letters XPISTOS. Christmas rose, signifying Messianic promise and nativity.

Epiphany Beginning January 6 (Epiphany Sunday) until Lent, including four to eight Sundays.

> Season of manifesting of Christ to all men, commemorating the visit of the Magi, who were Gentiles.

Color: Green for new life. Epiphany Day is white.

Symbol: Five-pointed star for Manifestation.

Pre-Easter or Lent   Begins forty days before Easter (*excluding* Sundays), on Ash Wednesday.

Season of fasting, representing penitence and self-discipline, enacting Christ's forty days in the wilderness, and culminating in the remembrance of His passion and death.

Color: purple for penitence. (Good Friday is black.)

Symbols: Ashes symbolize sorrow and repentance, Chalice and wafer for the Lord's Supper. Crown of thorns with three nails, Crucifix, Pointed cross of agony.

Easter and Post-Easter   (called *Eastertide* in some churches) Begins on Easter Sunday and continues for six more Sundays. Easter is the first Sunday after the first full moon that falls on or next after the spring equinox. The sun moving from south over the equator is usually between March 20 and 22.

Easter Dates:

1971 April 11

1972 April 2

1973 April 22

1974 April 14

1975 March 30

1976 April 18

1977 April 10

1978 March 26

1979 April 15

1980 April 6

Season is for celebrating the Resurrection, God's victory over sin and His gifts of grace and life in Jesus Christ.

Color: white for joy and victory.

Symbols: empty cross to signify the risen Lord; Lily, life from death; Phoenix, legendary bird, symbolizing life rising from ashes; pomegranate, power to reproduce life; peacock, growth of new feathers more brilliant than molted ones; butterfly, new, free life from old restricted cocoon.

Pentecost Begins seventh Sunday after Easter (Pentecost Sunday), extending to the last Sunday in August.

Season of God's gift of the Holy Spirit. Some churches call this season Trinity, others Whitsuntide.

Color: red for the blood of the martyrs and the fire of the Holy Spirit. The second Sunday (Trinity Sunday) is white in some churches, green is used for the remainder signifying new life and growth.

Symbol: Seven-tongued flame representing Pentecost; descending dove, for the descent of the Holy Spirit; seven lamps or seven-branched candlestick, symbolic of the seven gifts of the Holy Spirit—power, riches, wisdom, strength, honor, glory and blessing.

Kingdomtide Beginning last Sunday in August until Advent.

Season of eternal kingship of Christ in all phases of life, emphasizing the teachings of Jesus and the responsibilities of the Christian.

Color: green for new life and growth.

Symbol: Crown imposed on Cross, signifying kingship.

CALLS TO WORSHIP AND CELEBRATION

1

LEADER We come to worship, not because it is a duty
RESPONSE But because it is a delight;
LEADER Not because a minister calls us,

RESPONSE   But because God has called to us;
LEADER   Not to display to the world our fine garb,
RESPONSE   But to witness to the world our faith in God;
LEADER   Not to smirk at others because of our goodness,
RESPONSE   But to search together for God's righteousness;
LEADER   Not to be complimented for our proficiency,
RESPONSE   But to hear the Word speak to our deficiency;
LEADER   Not to listen as others are condemned,
RESPONSE   But to be told how we have sinned;
LEADER   Not to be satisfied with knowing religious rules,
RESPONSE   But to surrender all to the Kingdom's rule;
LEADER   Not to take away whatever God will give us,
RESPONSE   But to go away fitted for service;
UNISON   We would encounter the God who searches for us.

2

LEADER   Worship is the divine calling the human to come to the waters and drink. It is man hearing the call and coming to receive the water of life, so we come;
FIRST READER   As a thirsty land crying out for rain.
SECOND READER   As a sheep lost in the wilderness pleading for rescue by the Good Shepherd.
FIRST READER   As the same sheep nestled in the arms of his rescuer.
SECOND READER   As a hungry heart seeking for love.
LEADER   We hear the voice of our Father. O come, let us worship and bow down.

3

LEADER   Friends, we have come here to celebrate!
RESPONSE   Worship is the celebration of life. Worship is an expression of that which gives life and holds off death.
LEADER   Our celebration is focused on an event in the world.
RESPONSE   For us that one event is that in which God made himself known in his people Israel, in Jesus, and in his church.

UNISON   Oh, what joy has come! What a new outlook we now have! Thanks be to God forever.

4

LEADER   Worship is man's response to the nature of God as revealed in Jesus of Nazareth.

RESPONSE   Humbly we come in awe and gladness to express appreciation in every conceivable way.

LEADER   Worship acknowledges God's initiative in loving us, each one, even when we are unlovable and undeserving,

RESPONSE   With sensitive hearts we come in reverence, wonder and love to honor You, O God.

LEADER   Worship is communion between worshipers and God.

RESPONSE   We now enter into fellowship with God who has made us to think His thoughts, to feel His feelings, and to commune mind with mind, soul with soul.

5

LEADER   Come alive!

RESPONSE   Life is a complicated business bearing the promise of mystery and sunshine.

LEADER   You and I, with the Spirit of Christ, can help suns to rise in someone's life each new morning.

RESPONSE   Love is here to stay—that is enough!

LEADER   To believe in the God of Jesus is to be alive, and to know that there will be wonderful surprises.

6   3/11/64

LEADER   Worship is the submission of our nature to God.

RESPONSE   It is the quickening of conscience by His holiness,

LEADER   The nourishment of mind with His truth;

RESPONSE   The purifying of imagination by His beauty,

LEADER   The opening of the heart to His love,

RESPONSE   The surrender of the will to His purpose,

LEADER   O come, open your souls to the influence of God's Spirit.

7

LEADER   I call upon all of you here to join me in making a personal commitment.

RESPONSE   We are the body of Christ. Amen.

LEADER   The body needs our heart,

RESPONSE   Amen. Amen.

LEADER   As wholly as I can, I give to this fellowship in Christ my very heart and attention.

RESPONSE   Amen. Amen.

8

LEADER   God lights up men's hearts when they truly hear with the inner ear.

RESPONSE   Help us to search you out, O God.

LEADER   God does not speak with audible words, but in meanings, impressions and compulsions.

RESPONSE   Help us to listen, that through the music, readings, prayers, spoken words and the beauty of this place and other persons, we may hear.

LEADER   Let everybody be still.

RESPONSE   So we can hear God.

9

LEADER   Knock, Holy Spirit, upon the door of our hearts.

RESPONSE   In gratitude that makes us humble, in memory that makes us penitent, in vision that challenges our finest, in compassion that opens the gates of generosity.

UNISON   Come.

10

LEADER   Clap your hands all people!

RESPONSE   (*clap hands*)

LEADER   Shout to God with loud songs of joy!

RESPONSE   Amen, Amen, Amen.

LEADER   He made us, and everything we see.

RESPONSE   Praise be to God!

11

LEADER Good morning and welcome to a becoming people.

RESPONSE We are a becoming people, a people on the move.

LEADER We are moving up. We are moving out.

RESPONSE Up into a higher realm of humanness in our existence; out into a greater depth of humanness in our service.

12

LEADER Good morning, Christian friends. We are here this day to become one body in Christ.

RESPONSE Jesus promised, ". . . where two or three are gathered in my name, there am I in the midst of them" (Matthew 18:20).

LEADER Welcome, then. Let us worship the Lord of the Was, the Is Now and the Will Be. Amen.

RESPONSE May it be so.

13

LEADER Like the sun that is far away and yet close at hand to warm us, so God's Spirit is ever present and around us.

RESPONSE Grant us perspective and mystical ability to realize Your presence here.

LEADER Let not clouds of depression or doubt or guilt keep the waves of God's Spirit from us.

RESPONSE We open now the windows of our souls. Come Holy Spirit into our being. We live and move and have our very being in You.

14

You, who through worship would find God, know you not that God this very hour is seeking you? Lay before Him now, a mind open to all truth, senses alert to the beauty of His world, a spirit attuned to the whisper of the still small voice, a heart responsive to the cries of human needs, and a will committed to the walking of His way: then you shall go forth a soul renewed, exalted, ennobled, empowered, for our Great God is a Giver Supreme.

15

LEADER   My friends in Christ, we come together because of our common need for spiritual renewal.

RESPONSE   Let us worship God in such a way that He is able to renew us for and in His service.

LEADER   Grace to you and peace from God, the Father.

RESPONSE   Amen.

16

LEADER   We come here to worship:

FIRST READER   As a Prodigal running to his Father,

SECOND READER   As a soul standing in awe before the mystery of the universe,

FIRST READER   As a poet enthralled with the beauty of a sunrise,

SECOND READER   As a man listening through a tornado for the still small voice,

FIRST READER   As a drop of water in quest of the ocean,

SECOND READER   As Time flowing into Eternity,

FIRST READER   As a workman pausing to listen to a strain of music,

SECOND READER   As a child climbing into the lap of his father,

LEADER   O, come let us worship.

ADDRESSING GOD

O God, You are not present in just one place, or alive in just one time, because all times and places are in You. From this room and in this hour, we lift up our thoughts beyond all time and all space unto you, the uncreated One. . . .

O hidden Source of life, the uncreated mind behind all creation, the person in all personhood. . . .

Eternal One, whose presence is hidden behind the clothes of nature, who art the hand in the glove of the universe, to whom the trees and flowers are ornaments to accent the beauty of Your being. . . .

Soul of the Universe, what our head is to our body, You must be to all creation: the essence of personality, the center of consciousness, the energizer of life—and infinitely more.

Spirit of Life, love and beauty, You must indwell all creation as we indwell our body. No part is apart from You, and yet You are greater than any and all parts.

O Lord, not so much by logic, not alone as the "first cause" of what we see, rather in the character and being of persons, we know You, God, for we bear the image of Your being.

High and Eternal Goodness, who has reached through the stable door into our experience. . . .

O Ultimate Concern, produced neither by our will or intellect, but the producer of human compassion and love. . . .

Center of our commitment, the meaning of our seriousness, the clue to our existence. . . .

Infinite God, beyond the borders of our highest thoughts, beyond the edges of our sight, Your Being stretches, so we keep open the end of faith. . . .

O Living Christ, we confront You in the cry of the oppressed, as well as in the generous neighbor. . . .

O God, we do not know all there is to know about You, but we feel all we need to know is seen in Jesus. . . .

O Jesus, You are the window through which we see the real in reality. . . .

INVOCATIONS

1

O God, before whose knowledge all human hearts lie bare and open; let Your Spirit enter into us, so that new affections may enthrall us, new purposes involve us, and new dreams lure us, for Your kingdom's sake. Amen.

2

Through all the ages You have been the giver of life, the source of all knowledge, the fountain of all goodness, the enlightener of men's minds, and the Lord of history. We are thankful that we have been born in an age and in a nation that has known Your name and struggled for Your will, as known in Jesus, Your representative and our negotiator. Amen.

3

Here we are—with little power and less prestige—yet lifting up voices and feelings to You. You are hidden behind this curtain of sight, but we trust not removed from hearing our thoughts, instructing our minds, directing our energies and sustaining us in obedience and service, in Jesus' name. Amen.

4

Eternal Being, who existed before all things; whose intention is expressed in all things; who will endure beyond all things; symbolically we praise Thee in this service in the highest ways we know; for this magnificently organized universe in which You have housed us, for the heights and depths of Your purpose, and for Your love to us. Such knowledge is wonderful to think about. Glory be to Thee!

5

Like the living blood that flows through our bodies, so You, God, are present throughout the universe. Heaven and earth are full of You so none can hide himself from where You are not. Yet there is one place where we feel the pulse and know the heart is beating. It is here in this place where words and songs, readings and movements, sounds and lights, symbols and persons cause us to feel the beating of Your Spirit, as in Jesus Christ. Amen.

6

O Thou Beginner of our yesterdays, Mystery of our today, and Hope of our tomorrows we acknowledge in humility and gratitude our dependence, and praise Your Holy Name.

7

God, who must love all shades of color, whose love for beauty is seen in the psychedelic components of earth, by whose design the seasons parade with quiet majesty, whose harmony is seen in exquisite blends of autumn, we are limited in words to express the feelings of elation and sheer wonder as our spirits feast upon the beauty. How majestic is Thy name in all the earth. Heaven and earth are full of Thee.

8

Eternal Spirit, who out of the mysterious womb of nature has created us, with minds to see truth, hearts to respond to beauty, and wills to choose righteousness, we worship You as embodied in Jesus of human experience. Amen.

9

We are thankful for Jesus, who has shown us that behind the veil of our vision beats a heart of love. So we have come here with our troubles and sorrows that we might find light for our darkness, assurance for our doubts, and peace for our nerves.

10

God, You are greater than all our names given You; larger than all our human symbols describing You; closer than the person sitting next to us; and more real than we realize. So we come to express to You our adoration in as many ways as we can.

11

We bow in shuddering awe before the incredible mysteriousness of life that confronts us this day and in this place. We are humbled by the universe that overwhelms us; by beauty that enthralls us; a Providence that has provided for us; a love demonstration that melts us. O God, how marvelous and majestic and unexplainable are Your ways in all the earth. We worship You.

12

Special Easter Invocation We have bathed ourselves, fixed our hair, put on our newest and most attractive clothes and cologne so that we might be beautiful for You this day, God. We have come like civilized people, remembering our manners, treating one another and Your house with due respect. We're here to celebrate the victory. So accept the intentions of our minds, the joy of our voices, the praise from our lips as worthy of this Easter day and the love and power You displayed through Jesus our Lord. Amen.

PARAPHRASED SCRIPTURE

PSALM 23

The Lord is my friend!
What more could I want?
He sits with me in the quiet times of my days.
He explores with me the meanings of life.
He calls me forth as a whole person.
Even though I walk along paths of pain, prejudice, hatred, depression,
My fears are quieted
Because He is with me.
His words and His thoughts,
They challenge me.
He causes me to be sensitive to the needs of mankind,
Then lifts up opportunities for serving.
His confidence stretches me.
Surely love shall be mine to share throughout my life,
And I shall be sustained by His concern forever.[10]

PSALM 23
Psalm for Busy People

The Lord is my Pacesetter, I shall not rush,
He makes me stop and rest for quiet intervals,

He provides me with images of stillness, which restore my
serenity.
He leads me in ways of efficiency; through calmness of mind,
And His guidance is peace.
Even though I have a great many things to accomplish each day
I will not fret, for His presence is here,
His timelessness, His all-importance will keep me in balance.
He prepares refreshment and renewal in the midst of my activity
By anointing my mind with His oils of tranquility.
My cup of joyous energy overflows.
Surely harmony and effectiveness shall be the fruits of my hours,
For I shall walk in the pace of my Lord, and dwell in His house
forever.[11]

PSALM 1

Happy is that person who does not take advice from question-
able sources; who does not keep company with the disreputable
or join with malicious scoffers.

Rather, happy is the person who finds his satisfaction and joy
in the Lord. He studies and meditates upon God's will for the
day and for the night.

That person shall have deep roots like the tree, which reaches
down into running streams of water. Such a tree is always alive,
beautifully green, and blossoms with fruit at the proper season.
So is the deeply rooted person, and men shall know him by his
good works.

However, the wicked have no roots, hence no stability or good
works. So, like fallen leaves, they are blown hither and yon by
the prevailing wind.

The evil-intentioned person will not be able to hold up in the
time of trial, nor be respected or approved in the company of
the righteous.

God will vindicate the ways of righteousness, but the ways of
evil ultimately will be frustrated and fade from sight.

PSALM 100

All lands of people sing joyful praises to the God of our life.
Serve in His spirit with happiness; worship Him with active
enthusiasm and vocal participation.

Acknowledge God as the producer and soul of the universe. He
fathered our spiritual nature, so we are kin to Him. We are His
people, His creation, His family.

Then, in thoughtful gratitude, enter the sanctuary dedicated
to His worship to declare your dependence upon Him, and your
humble praise for His undeserved goodness. Utter words of
thanks that reveal the genuine value in which you regard Him,
and the reverence by which you respect His name.

God and His love will last forever. He will be equally faithful to all generations of people.

PSALM 86

Put your ear next to me, Lord,
I just want you to hear me and talk to me
'Cause I ain't got much.
Just remember I try to be like you
You are my man
So I ask for your help.
Make me happy when I'm mixed up inside.
We know you don't hold nothing against us
And you listen and hear us when we talk to you
And don't push us away.
So when we got troubles
We can call up you.

Help us remember you is only one
And everybody was made by you
And had sure better know it
And you are the only God.

Show me the right side of the street to walk on
So I can walk with you and even trust you
And not be afraid to say it
'Cause your love is just great.

When it seems like everybody is against me
And nothing goes right
And people is out to get me
Help me to know we is still friends
And that your love is here.
That's what helps me have heart.
So "give me some skin," Lord,
Then everybody will know where we stand.[12]

PSALM 15

O Lord, who shall live in your house?
Who shall stick around your yard?
The one who pulls no jobs and does right
And levels with you
And the one who plays it straight
And who sticks by his friend and don't go up on other people
And the one who hates rotten things
And who trusts God's friends.
And who always stands true
And not the loan sharks
And not the squealers.
And all that's for sure
And this will always be so.[13]

JOHN 1

Before anything came into existence, God existed as the life-giving, creative spirit. In His mind were all the ideas of creation; apart from His thought, nothing came into being.

To communicate to man His supreme creation, His thoughts about life's purposes and meaning and the reality of being, He used various mediums.

Words became a vehicle for transferring what was in God's mind, into the mind of His offspring.

In the fullness of time, all of His thoughts were embodied into one Living *Word*—a Person. He became Truth in a body, personified. When this Person walked, behaved and lived before men, they got the ideas God was communicating.

A man named John experienced the light, and went about telling the *Word,* witnessing to it. He, himself, was not the *Living Word,* but he came to convey the Word so that others might experience the light of it. All men are made to respond to that light.

But some, so used to the darkness, were insensitive to the light. They rejected the Living Word, even some who lived with Him refused to believe Him.

JOHN 1:1–5, 14

In the beginning was the Idea, and the Idea was with God, and the Idea was divine. All things were made in pursuance of that Idea and without it nothing was made. The Idea was the sustaining Substance, the Inner Reality of all that was made.

The Idea became alive and the Life of it was the Light of men, the true Light that lights every man that comes into the world. The Idea was made flesh and dwelt among us full of grace and truth. No man has seen God at any time, but no man having once seen that Life full of grace and truth can fail to catch the Idea.

MATTHEW 5:1–13

One harvest day Jesus called us and His other friends to the hills. The earth was fragrant, and like the daughter of a king at her wedding feast, she wore all her jewels. And the sky was her bridegroom.

When we reached the heights Jesus stood still in the grove of laurels, and He said, "Rest here, quiet your mind and tune your heart, for I have much to tell you."

Then we reclined on the grass, and the summer flowers were all about us, and Jesus sat in our midst. And Jesus said:

"Blessed are the serene in spirit.

Blessed are they who are not held by possessions, for they shall be free.

Blessed are they who remember their pain, and in their pain await their joy.

Blessed are they who hunger after truth and beauty, for their hunger shall bring bread, and their thirst cool water.

Blessed are the kindly, for they shall be consoled by their own kindliness.

Blessed are the pure in heart, for they shall be one with God.

Blessed are the merciful, for mercy shall be in their portion.

Blessed are the peacemakers, for their spirit shall dwell above the battle, and they shall turn the potter's field into a garden.

Blessed are they who are hunted, for they shall be swift of foot and they shall be winged.

Rejoice and be joyful, for you have found the kingdom of heaven within you. The singers of old were persecuted when they sang of that kingdom. You too shall be persecuted, and therein lies your honor, and therein your reward." [14]

MATTHEW 25:14–30

Certain parents had three sons. One was endowed with outstanding ability, the second with average talent, but the third had below average capacities.

The parents reared their children well, providing education and every incentive so that each boy might realize his fullest potential.

The exceptionally gifted lad did very well developing his abilities. As he did so, other capacities were realized. Many opportunities came his way for using his life beneficially and constructively. He married happily and became father of fine children. He was given responsible positions, won a broad reputation, and brought honor and joy to his parents.

The second son, though not as gifted, nonetheless applied himself industriously. He did his very best, and though his positions were not as significant nor prestigious as his older brother, yet he was a blessing to his community. He made his parents very glad and happy, because he did the best he was capable of doing.

However, the third son felt totally inferior to his more illustrious and gifted brothers. He could never do what they had done. He resented his limitations. So, he did not try to apply himself nor better his skills. He withdrew, satisfied to retain what he had.

But as the years passed, he even lost what little he had, for abilities unused become abilities lost.

None are equally endowed, but equal dedication is expected of all. God does not judge us upon the degrees of our ability, but by what we do with what we have.

MATTHEW 25:35–46

I was hungry, and you formed a humanities club and discussed my hunger. Thank you.

I was imprisoned, and you crept off quietly to your chapel in the cellar and prayed for my release.

I was naked, and in your mind you debated the morality of my appearance.

I was sick, and you knelt and thanked God for your health.

I was homeless, and you preached to me of the spiritual shelter of the love of God.

I was lonely, and you left me alone to pray for me.

You seem so holy; so close to God.
But I'm still very hungry, and lonely, and cold.
So where have your prayers gone?
What have they done?
What does it profit a man to page through his book of prayers
   when the rest of the world is crying for help? [15]

LUKE 6:39–42

Can a blind man help another blind man across
the street?
   They both might get killed, right?
      Well you're not as smart as your teach',
         But if you listen, someday you might be
         And know as much as the teach'.
Why does it bug you so much when you see
   Something wrong with another guy
      When you ain't so hot yourself?
So when you talk big, man, we say, "Look, who's
talking."
   How can you help another guy,
      When you're the one who needs some help?
Why don't you wise up?
   First get yourself fixed up
      And fly straight,
         Then people won't say
            "Look, who's talking." [16]

LUKE 10:33–37

A man was going down from his apartment in the project to
his friend's house. While he was walking, a couple of muggers
jumped him in a dark place. He didn't have very much, so they
took his wallet and clothes and beat on him and stomped on him
—they almost killed him.

Before long a hood came by, but he didn't give a care. Besides, the cops might ask him questions, so he beat it out of there. Next came a squeak—never gave the poor guy a second look. After a while a real cool square comes along. He sees the character, feels sorry for him. So he puts a couple of band-aids on, gives him a drink, and a lift in his car. The square even put him up in a room some place. Cost him two bucks, too!

So who do you think the best guy was? Well, you got the message, bud. But you don't have to be a square to show love, and to be sorry for someone, and to help a guy. But get with it, man—this is what God wants you to do.[17]

JOHN 14:1-3

When death invades your circle, do not feel forlorn or filled with despair. If you will believe in God as I have shown you, you can be at peace. This universe is His house, and it has many rooms. The earth with its beauty is one room; there are other rooms. He is evident in them all.

Death is a door opening from one room to another. The rooms are not unprepared as though left without provisions.

You have experienced, then trusted the provisions of earth for this room of existence. You can rely upon the provisions in the future room as well.

If it were untrue, I would be the first to know and to tell you. I have founded the highest system of ethics the people of earth have ever known. You can have confidence in this assurance, because it is more than the fickle promises of the systems and opinions of men. It is the trust that fills the heart with perfect peace.

ROMANS 8:35-39

When we are identified with God through the spirit, work and meaning of Jesus, is there anything that can take us beyond the love of God? Can we ever drift beyond the limits of His concern? Is it really possible to be beyond God's ability to help us? Can our indifference, ingratitude, rebellious sin, or callousness ever change God's feelings for us?

I am as sure of this as I am that the moon is in the sky, that nothing in life, no creatures in creation, no handicaps, no misfortunes, no tempting pleasures, not even death itself, can take us where God's love is not evident and available.

Therefore, friends, be confident, assured and stable through all the vicissitudes of life. Invest yourself in those qualities which endure beyond the horizons of time.

ROMANS 12

Because of God's goodness to you, Christian friends, I urge you to use your bodies in dedicated service which God approves. Do not allow the patterns of secular people to mold you into their ways, but be different by the inner conditioning of your thoughts. Only then can you demonstrate unquestionable behavior and what is the true will of God.

Since we are all recipients of undeserved love and are, in a sense, dependent upon God's mercy, let no person have an exaggerated opinion of himself, rather let him have confidence in his personal value because of the evidence of worth by God's love.

The human body has many parts, and each has its unique function, performing in intricate coordination with all other parts. The church is like a body for doing Christ's will. We as parts of Christ's body, are united in Him. Each has a unique function to perform, depending upon his particular abilities given of God.

If you have ability to analyze and predict the future, do so with positive faith. If you have abilities to teach or counsel, to preach or lead, do so with concentration. If you are blessed with material wealth, be a liberal giver. If you have the ability to comfort and heal and to be compassionate, do so with joy.

Let your love be true. Cling tenaciously to what is good, while refusing absolutely all evil. In relationships with others, show tender concern; be warm spirited and respectful; continue to pray regularly; keep communications open, especially with the godly, and be hospitable. Share the joy of those who are joyful, and enter vicariously into the sorrow of those who weep.

Have the same attitude toward everyone. Do not feel aloof and superior to lowly tasks or common people or things as though you were conceited. Give attention to what is honorable. Seek no retaliation when unjustly abused, for vengeance belongs to God alone. Let Him punish and you can be sure He will. So far as your actions are concerned, be peaceful with all men. If an offender is hungry or thirsty, arrange food for him; this will soften his feelings toward you. In this way enemies may be turned into friends. So, be careful not to be overcome by evil. You overcome evil by doing good.

I CORINTHIANS 12:12–13:13

Just as a team is a unit but has many players and all the players on the team—even though there are many of them—make up one team, so it is with Christ. For by one Spirit we all were selected for this squad—whether American or European, Caucasian or Negro—and all have been inspired by the one Spirit.

For the team does not consist of one player, but of many. If the guard should say, "Because I am not an end, I do not belong to the team," that would not make him any less a member of the team.

If the outfielder should say, "Because I am not a pitcher, I do not belong to the team," he would still be a necessary member of the team. If the whole team were pitchers, who would cover third? If the whole team were halfbacks, who would snap the ball? But as it is, God has arranged positions on the team according to the rules of the game. If everybody played the same position where would the team be? So there are many positions but only one team. The quarterback cannot say to the tackle, "Who needs you?" Nor the forward to the guard, "Get lost." On the contrary, the positions which may seem to be inconspicuous may really be indispensable.

Now you are a team for Christ. Each of you is a team member. And God has assigned different positions to be played. So you are certainly wise to desire the finest skills.

I will show you a more excellent way. If I can play many sports but have not love, I am merely a flashy player. If I know all about athletics, and have the skill to become a coach, but have not love, I am just a nobody. If I really give all I've got to being an outstanding player, and have not love, my score is zero.

Then what is love? Love is a combination of many attitudes, like patience, kindness, like considering the other person's point of view, like not being glad when somebody drops out, but being glad when he makes good.

There are three basic skills for living: faith, hope, and love. But the greatest of these is love.[18]

I CORINTHIANS 13:1–7

Though you speak with tongues of men and of angels and have not human understanding, you are a noisy gong or a clanging cymbal. And though you can explain the Scriptures in learned fashion and quote from the latest commentaries with complete assurance, even if you master the art of holding twelve-year-old boys spellbound as you expound the Minor Prophets, and still have not human understanding, you are nothing. If you put every penny (and dollar, too) into the offering plate each Sunday morning, if you work in the church kitchen every time there is a supper, if you learn to call all members of your congregation by their first names, yea, even if you come into the House of God each time its doors are opened, and have not human understanding, you gain nothing.

Understanding is patient, kind, not jealous of another's good fortune, not self-exalting, or rude. Understanding does not insist on its own way, is not irritable, or resentful. It is touched by sadness when someone else has unhappiness, and finds great delight in another's good fortune. Human understanding is able to take whatever happens, always believing the best of people. Human understanding never, never gives up in reaching out with compassion.[19]

HEBREWS 12:1-2

We are surrounded by a great host of persons both present and invisible, who are greatly interested in us. They could well be likened to the grandstand spectators at a track meet. We are the runners in the race called Life. We compete not with one another, but strive toward the world record for living held by Jesus. So, let us take off our warm-up suits and jewelry, and dress as simple and lightly as possible so we will not be hindered in any way. Then let us run with perseverance, concentrating upon the mark of perfection as it is in Jesus Christ.

MODERN LIVING PARABLES
AND READINGS

GREATER LOVE HAS NO MAN

The incidents of which we were hearing now impressed us profoundly.

One that went the rounds soon after concerned another Argyll. He was in a work detail on the railroad.

The day's work had ended; the tools were being counted. When the party was about to be dismissed the Japanese guard declared that a shovel was missing. He insisted someone had stolen it to sell to the Thais. He strode up and down in front of the men, ranting and denouncing them for their wickedness, their stupidity, and most unforgivable of all, their ingratitude to the Emperor.

Screaming in broken English, he demanded that the guilty one step forward to take his punishment. No one moved. The guard's rage reached new heights of violence.

"All die! All die!" he shrieked.

To show that he meant what he said, he pulled back the bolt, put the rifle to his shoulder, and looked down the sights, ready to fire at the first man he saw at the end of them. At that moment the Argyll stepped forward, stood stiffly at attention, and said calmly,

"I did it."

The guard unleashed all his whipped-up hatred; he kicked the hapless prisoner and beat him with his fists. Still the Argyll stood rigidly at attention. The blood was streaming down his face, but he made no sound. His silence goaded the guard to an excess of rage. He seized his rifle by the barrel and lifted it high over his head. With a final howl he brought the butt down on the skull of the Argyll, who sank limply to the ground and did not move. Although it was perfectly evident that he was dead, the guard continued to beat him and stopped only when exhausted.

The men of the work detail picked up their comrade's body, shouldered their tools, and marched back to camp. When the tools were counted again at the guardhouse no shovel was missing.[20]

ERNEST GORDON

THE SINGERS OF LIFE

[One day Loren Eiseley leaned against a stump at the edge of a small glade and fell asleep.]

When I awoke, dimly aware of some commotion and outcry in the clearing, the light was slanting down through the pines in such a way that the glade was lit like some vast cathedral. I could see the dust motes of wood pollen in the long shaft of light, and there on the extended branch sat an enormous raven with a red and squirming nestling in his beak.

The sound that awoke me was the outraged cries of the nestling's parents, who flew helplessly in circles about the clearing. The sleek black monster was indifferent to them. He gulped, whetted his beak on the dead branch a moment and sat still. Up to that point the little tragedy had followed the usual pattern. But suddenly, out of all that area of woodland, a soft sound of complaint began to rise. Into the glade fluttered small birds of half a dozen varieties drawn by the anguished outcries of the tiny parents.

No one dared to attack the raven. But they cried there in some instinctive common misery. The bereaved and the unbereaved. The glade filled with their soft rustling and their cries. They fluttered as though to point their wings at the murderer. There was a dim intangible ethic he had violated, that they knew. He was a bird of death.

And he, the murderer, the black bird at the heart of life, sat on there, glimmering in the common light, formidable, unmoving, unperturbed, untouchable.

The sighing died. It was then I saw the judgment. It was the judgment of life against death. I will never see it again so forcefully presented. I will never hear it again in notes so tragically prolonged. For in the midst of protest, they forgot the violence. There, in that clearing, the crystal note of a song sparrow lifted hesitantly in the hush. And finally, after painful fluttering, another took the song, and then another, the song passing from one bird to another, doubtfully at first, as though some evil thing were being slowly forgotten. Till suddenly they took heart and sang from many throats joyously together as birds are known to sing. They sang because life is sweet and sunlight beautiful.

They sang under the brooding shadow of the raven. In simple truth they had forgotten the raven, for they were the singers of life, and not of death.[21]

LOREN EISELEY

I HOLD THE BANDAGES AND OINTMENTS READY

I see my son is wearing long trousers, I tremble at this;

I see he goes forward confidently, he does not know so fully his own gentleness.

Go forward, eager and reverent child, see here I begin to take my hands away from you.

I shall see you walk careless on the edges of the precipice, but if you wish you shall hear no word come out of me;

My whole soul will be sick with apprehension, but I shall not disobey you.

Life sees you coming, she sees you come with assurance towards her.

She lies in wait for you, she cannot but hurt you;

Go forward, go forward, I hold the bandages and ointments ready,

And if you would go elsewhere and lie alone with your wounds, why, I shall not intrude upon you,

If you would seek the help of some other person, I shall not come forcing myself upon you.

If you should fall into sin, innocent one, that is the way of this pilgrimage;

Struggle against it, not for one fraction of a moment concede its dominion.

It will occasion you grief and sorrow, it will torment you,

But hate not God, nor turn from Him in shame or self-reproach;

He has seen many such, His compassion is as great as His Creation.

Be tempted and fall and return, return and be tempted and fall

A thousand times and a thousand, even to a thousand thousand. For out of this tribulation there comes a peace, deep in the soul, and surer than any dream.[22]

FROM A PERSONAL LETTER

What a horrid thing fear is—it keeps us apart from life instead of participating in it and causes us to waste so much of our God-given time on earth. To "have a go" is the important thing isn't it—not whether or not we succeed . . . When I sum up everything my short life has taught me . . . one thing I'm sure of, if we do faithfully the tasks which come to our hand from day to day, without thinking them either too big or too small, and if we take what life sends, without inquests, or too many "Why me's" . . . we may one day earn the privilege of being called a servant of the Lord and enter into the joys of true service. (Written by a dying cancer patient)

DILEMMA

We are caught in war, wanting peace. We are torn by division, wanting unity. We see around us empty lives, wanting fulfilment. We see tasks that need doing, waiting for hands to do them. To a crisis of the spirit, we need an answer of the spirit.

RICHARD M. NIXON, Inaugural Address

A PARABLE OF CHRISTMAS

A pastor in East Germany has written a play entitled the *Sign of Jonah*. These words have come to mean the Judgment of God upon men, alluding to the occasion when Jonah preached the Judgment of God upon the city of Nineveh. This play speaks with unusual power on some major issues of our day. It has inspired many attempts to lift up some special part of the drama and to adapt it to different uses. It inspired Andrew T. L. Armstrong to suggest the following Christmas parable.

At the end of time, all the people who ever lived were brought before God to be judged for their life on earth. They were assembled together on a great plain before God's throne. It was an unusual crowd, however. They were not submissive. Instead, they clustered here and there talking heatedly with one another. They weren't acting as you might expect they should: with genuine shame for wrongs they had done on earth. Quite the contrary was the case.

One of the groups was composed of the *Jews* who had suffered persecution from men. The great number of them—in the millions—were the Jews who died in the Nazi concentration camps. These asked, "What can God know of how we have suffered? We know what it is to be despised and treated with hatred. We were starved, beaten, and finally tortured to death."

Another of the groups was made up of *American Negroes*. They too questioned God's right to judge them. Just look at what He had allowed to happen to them. Their people had been taken slaves, carried from their homeland into a strange country. Thousands had died in suffocating slave ships. The survivors suffered all kinds of indignities from the white men. And their children were forced into second-class position by people who thought they were God's chosen people.

Another group consisted of all the children who had been born *out of wedlock*. Each bore on his forehead the stamp ILLEGITIMATE. Many of them knew neither their father nor mother. They had endured the stigma of doubtful ancestry all their life. They, too, wanted to know when God ever had to endure what they had suffered.

Far out across the plain were hundreds of such groups. Each had a complaint against God for the evil and suffering He permitted in His world. How lucky God was to live in heaven where all was sweetness and light——where there was no *weeping*, no *fear,* no *hunger* or *hatred, indeed,* what *did* God know of what man had been forced to endure in this world He had made? After all, God leads a sheltered life, they said.

So each of these groups sent forth a leader, chosen because he had suffered the most. Among them was a *Jew,* a *Negro,* and an *untouchable* from India. The fourth was a horribly deformed *arthritic.* There were, also, one from *Hiroshima* and one from a *Siberian Slave Camp.* There in the center of the plain, before the throne of God, they consulted with each other.

At last they were ready to present their case. It was rather simple. Before God would be qualified to be their judge, He must endure what they had endured. Their decision was that *God should be sentenced to live on earth—as a man!* Because He was God, they had set certain safeguards to be sure He could not use His divine powers to help Him. So they pronounced His sentence:

> *Let him be born a Jew.*
> *Let the legitimacy of his birth be doubted, so that no one will know who is really his father. Thus he can inherit nothing.*
> *Give him a work so difficult, that even his family will think he is out of his mind when he tries to do it. Let him try to describe what no man has ever seen, tasted, heard, or smelled. Let him try to describe God to man.*
> *Let him be rejected by the very people who worship him.*
> *Let him be betrayed by his dearest friends.*
> *Let him be indicted on false charges, tried like them before a prejudiced jury, and convicted by a cowardly judge.*
> *At last—let him see what it means to be terribly alone, completely abandoned by his friends.*
> *Let him be tortured.*
> *Then, let him die! Let him die so that there can be no doubt that he died, and that he was dead. Let there be a great host of witnesses to verify it.*

As each leader announced his sentence of God, loud murmurs of approval went up from the great throng of people on the open plain. When the last had finished pronouncing sentence, there was a long silence. Those who had pronounced their judgment of God quietly departed. No one uttered a word—or made a sound. No one moved. For then, suddenly, they all knew—*God had already served His sentence!*

> [For unto us a son is given, unto us a child is born,]
>   and his name shall be called Em-
>   măn' ū ėl
>   (which means, God with us) (Matthew 1:23).

> The people who walked in darkness
>   have seen a great light (Isaiah 9:2).

> And being found in human form he
>   humbled himself and became obedient
>   unto death, even death on a cross (Philippians 2:8).

This is the meaning of the Parable of Christmas. This is the truth of Christmas: That He, too, has gone this way, and hereafter, no one needs to walk alone.

FREEDOM

Freedom . . . is inwardness, spontaneity, the capacity of a man to find within himself the reasons and the motives of his own right decisions and actions, apart from external coercion. Freedom therefore is authenticity, truthfulness, fidelity to the pursuit of truth and to the truth when found. In further consequence, freedom is experienced as duty, as responsibility, as a response to the claims of justice, to the demands of rightful law, to the governance and guidance of legitimate authority. In its intimately Christian sense, however, freedom has a higher meaning than all of this. Freedom, in the deepest experience of all, is love. To be free is to be for-the-others. The Christian call to freedom is inherently a call to community, a summons out of isolation, an invitation to be-with-others, an impulse to service of the others.[23]

THE LANGUAGE OF THE SOUL

When God created man, he gave him music as a language different from all other languages. Music is one of the vocabularies of the soul. With its gentle fingers, the doors to our feelings are opened, awakening memories that have long lain hidden in the files of the past. Pictures canvas the mind when painted by poetic lyrics. Moods are determined, in part at least, by varied sounds: trumpets call to action, strings soothe, percussion stirs the muscles. Sad strains of music make us weep; sweet notes make us smile. With eyes of our hearing, we see into the hidden heart of love. With music the hearts of kings have been melted and the calloused have been softened. Music has inspired poets, writers, dreamers and architects, and all that is finest within is stirred, heartened and strengthened. Our souls are like tender flowers at the mercy of the day's breezes. Man with his understanding does not know what the breeze is saying as it whistles through the trees, nor what the dancing waters are murmuring, nor what the bird sings as it awakens the night from slumber. But the heart of man can see and feel and grasp the meaning of these sounds that play upon his feelings. God speaks to man in this mysterious language. And man is made to see with his ears, and to hear with his heart, and to respond with his emotions. It is the only universal language; all mortals are created to understand. In it is our unity with God and fellow men, for music is the language of the soul.

O Divine Wisdom, speak to us through the language of music.

THE HEART OF WISDOM

Knowledge and wisdom are not the same. Knowledge is the accumulation of facts; wisdom is the correlation of these facts for the good of life. Knowledge is information, whereas wisdom has the ability to see perspective with deeper dimensions. There are many who are knowledgeable; few who are wise.

This is why the Psalmist said, ". . . get a heart of wisdom" (90:12), and Job recorded, ". . . the price of wisdom is above rubies" (28:18 KJV).

A man's worth lies in his wisdom, not in his wealth; in his deeds, not in his color, race, creed, or descent. The son of a farmer who possesses wisdom is of greater worth to a community or nation than the son of nobility who lacks common sense. A nation's true wealth is not in her bank accounts or production lines, but in the quality of her people. Wisdom is the true stature of greatness and earns nobility, irrespective of who one's father may be, or from what race he comes.

Wisdom is the only treasure that none can take from you. It gives you understanding, and in this is stability, for it will never prove untrue. Men will seek out the wise man, for his wisdom is like a candle illuminating the darkness, and it provides light for the path of mankind.

IT WAS JUST A DREAM

I had a dream last night; I dreamed that I was taken to the court of the Emperor of all the World. I knelt before Him and pleaded that the spirit of Christmas might be spread over all the Earth. He smiled sadly and said, "What would you have me do, my son?" My words poured out profusely—I knew what lighted Christmas trees, loaded baskets and angelic choirs would mean to the half-starved, empty-spirited children I had seen all over Asia. Imagine my joy when He granted my request: Christmas trees covered with tinsel were placed on every corner of every city, town and hamlet in the world, the air was filled with music and no one was hungry any more.

I looked down upon the world—the world which my plea had made full of Christmas, and I said, "It is good." The voice of the kindly Emperor said, "Look more closely, and tell me, is it good?"

Through heavenly binoculars, standing on the corner of the

Universe, I gazed down the long avenue of time—my heart fell—could my eyes be deceiving me or was that man tearing a branch from that Christmas tree to strike his neighbor? Did I hear aright: Was that church member calling his servant a "dirty coon?" Could it be true that the pretty Yuletide lights were going out because of a strike in which Labor and Capital were both guilty of tyrannical methods? Was that so-called Christian nation marshalling its armies for war once more? Softly the Emperor spoke, "My son, Christmas in itself means very little. If the people on the earth would read my book of life more carefully, they would see that humble shepherds on Judean hills, choirs of angels, a lowly manger, a glowing star and wise men bringing rich gifts are only half the picture. I have also revealed that always there is a Herod in the background who rides roughshod over Christmas trees. His voice is louder than even my ten-thousand-voiced choir and he is always present, trying to kill every Christ-child before it becomes two years of age. My son, you made the wrong request. You do not want Christmas over all the world—you want the Christ in every heart and even I, with all my power, cannot force my children to open their hearts to Him. Another thing, my son, in our effort to Christianize human-ity, we have tried to make it authoritarian. We have, through the ages, streamlined it to reduce wind resistance by saying, '*Believe this creed*' instead of, '*Live this life.*' My Christ-child, whom I placed in the manger, did not want adherence to a creed—He wanted allegiance to His spirit. He did not want His church to be a museum for the exhibition of perfect Christians. He wanted it to be a hospital for the making of better ones."

This statement burned my consciousness into wakefulness, and I awoke with a feeling of doom and walked out under the stars. The night was hushed and my heart cried quietly within me, and then I prayed as I had never prayed before.

> Emperor of all men—
> Help me to help others and myself to see,
> That Christmas depends on the likes of me.

That it isn't far to Bethlehem town;
That it's anywhere that Christ comes down;
That charters of freedom and bills of right
Are merely the symbols of some great lights—
That men accepted through ages past
When they found that truth alone would last.
Help us, O God, like these shepherdmen,
To follow the star that shines again
On a hungry, embittered and tired world
To carry the banner bravely unfurled—
Of justice and brotherhood, love and peace
Of kindly compassion that never will cease,
And most of all, O God, show us the light
Which came to unite the world one Holy Night.[24]

CONTEMPORARY PRAYERS FOR PASTORS

1

Here we sit, in this place removed from the routine of business and the emptiness of daily routine, to think about You, God. If we could catch You in our nets, if we could run out thoughts around Your being, then You would be no greater than we are. So we feel a sense of wonder, humility, and reverence, and bow before Your greatness and mystery.

Why are we here? What is life all about? Why have You designed us? In the midst of our days that melt away like snowflakes, we turn to You so that we might see our life against the backdrop of Your being. If You have no plan, our building is vain. Only in Your eternalness and purposes does our life have meaning. So throw Your greatness about our littleness. Be our stability and permanency amid the anxieties of time. Help us to know that underneath are everlasting arms that will never let down.

How come we have been born in this good land? Free from the lot of so many who are homeless, or starving, or enslaved? When we are quiet we can hear their stomachs growl and their hearts cry. Beyond all lines of nation and race, our sympathy goes out to them today. O God, awaken compassion, justice, and peace beginning with us. Amen.

2

Mysterious God—we know You exist. True, we cannot put You in a test tube, or isolate You like we do objects or other persons. We cannot stand back and observe You like a star or tree. Still we know You as the source of goodness and order; as the ground of being; as the personality in personhood; as the love in relationships. We have experienced Your presence, God, and we know You intuitively.

Nevertheless, we find it difficult to describe who You are. We know we can never completely master You with our human minds. We would like help so You could be more real. We would like to develop our spiritual, mystical nature so we could be authentic human beings in Your likeness. We would pray to be more Christlike.

In this way, Divine Father of Creation, we can be Your witnesses. We can be channels of Your grace. Forgive us for allowing our humanness, our natural man, to block the flow of Your peace.

In Your love may we bridge the gap between the generations, nations and races to be reconciled through Jesus Christ. Amen.

3

God, we are believers, yet we find it difficult to pray, and to know You. We would like help so You could be a more real relationship to us.

Would it be all right to think of You as we think of our own selves? Are You outside physical creation, in the same way we transcend our bodies in thoughts, self-evaluations, dreams and memory? We are not limited to our abode for in thought we can be anywhere. Perhaps You are "inside" creation in the way we "permeate and influence" our body. Could this be so—except infinitely more so?

We like to think of You as the spirit of love, the wisdom of meaning, the conscious in consciousness, the justice in truth, the holiness in beauty. Where these are, You are or have been.

I guess Jesus sums You up best, God. In fact, we cannot really think of You without thinking of a love like Jesus', compassion like Jesus', spirit like Jesus'. Our faith and knowledge of You seems to begin and end in Jesus. Since we know Him, we know You. We feel great about it. Amen.

4

Sweet Mystery of Life, at last we have found You! Vainly have we searched to know the secret that holds life together, that makes sense. Earnestly have we searched to know You who are beyond definition, beyond ability to capture and confine, beyond all. Now at last we have found You where You have been seeking us all along, in the beauty, love and truth of Jesus Christ. We rejoice!

We have been accustomed to think of You, God, as "out there," above the stars, as a giant in the far off sky, in another world. Now to think we have met You in person, in the common humanity in us that meets the humanity in another, in the Christlikeness in another's spirit. O God, we understand now! The mystery is solved. As we do not seek the sun, only open ourselves to its warmth and light, so may we be open to Your presence. Down the stairway, into the humble place of our inner being where we live, enter now, dear Friend. You are no longer mystery. Amen.

5

Lord, we are here today—in this place—not to try to escape from this community's problems, though we would like to! O God, how we would like to! We would like to withdraw into an ivory tower, a safe distance away, behind high walls; then close our eyes and our ears and our minds, and forget the turmoil and war, strikes and campus revolutions. We would like to not be reminded of poverty and squalor, pain and death and pretend it does not exist. If we could just go about our own pursuits uninterrupted and unconcerned. But God, we can't!

Even now we know the unreasonable demands, threats and the violence are but the cries of frustrated, unhappy, impatient people—and we must listen. O Lord, You know the ill-flavored words that have been hurled, the bitterness and jealousy that has poisoned life. Tempers are jagged and explosive. Lord, this city is like a keg of dynamite with the fuse ignited. There could be a terrible outbreak of bloodshed right here in this city. Lord, we've come here to get our calm, to gain perspective, to pray for honesty enough to see and admit injustice; to plead for wisdom to know what should be done, and courage to urge it to be done. Above all, Lord, we're Your "new humanity" that You have created to be peacemakers and reconcilers. Then, guide our thoughts by Your thoughts and our spirits by Jesus' spirit, so that our actions might be Your actions, in the name of peace. Amen.

6

LEADER   Sometimes prayer is the plea of an employer.

AN EMPLOYER FROM THE CONGREGATION   Lord, I feel handicapped. All week I have been out of joint at the office. Yesterday I came unglued when my work was criticized. Jobs and people come at me on jet wings, and at such a speed I lose perspective. All the little things become too great, and great things slip into insignificance. It is so hard to be stable in this crazy world. O God, let me take another squint at Your blueprint for me.

LEADER   Sometimes prayer is the plea of a youth.

YOUTH FROM THE CONGREGATION   Lord, my folks and I don't get along too well. Was I shortchanged on patience, or are they long shots on hope? When I break a little rule, they make a federal case. When I follow the rule they take it for granted. Lord, I am glad for my parents—they are great. It just seems they expect too much. "Honor thy father and mother" should carry a footnote, "Give the kids a break."

LEADER   Sometimes prayer is confession.

CHURCH MEMBER FROM THE CONGREGATION   Lord, I want to be Your child, but I keep losing my way. I want to take time to read the Bible and to pray, but duty calls and I find myself racing the clock. I thirst after righteousness but then I forget to stop at the well with my cup. I try to be a good citizen of Your kingdom, but my courage and strength run away at the first encounter. O God, do not let me dwell on excuses. Turn my eyes to opportunities whereby I may drink deeply of Your spirit and serve more meaningfully in Your love.

LEADER   Sometimes prayer is simply a mood with no words at all.

CONGREGATION   (*In creative silence.*)

7

O God, You know the desperate and relentless struggles of persons known or unknown to us who need immediate help. Believing that You are able to do much more than we can ask or think and that You respond to the wave lengths of our concerns and intercession, we place upon the altar for Your blessings these persons. (*a period of silence after each request*)

Pray for:

A bereft soul for whom the heavens seem shut.

A daughter who has sacrificed her future and chances of marriage for the care of a widowed mother.

A used car salesman torn between the ethical requirements of the Gospel and the demands of his employer to meet ruthless competition.

Anxious parents who have not heard from an absent child for two months or more—a daughter gone to work in a distant city, a son drafted into military service and now in Viet Nam, the youngest of their family away in college.

A clerk whose financial needs tempt him to filch from the cash register.

A stenographer whose job depends on humoring the whims of an amorous boss.

A man under cancer's death sentence.

A mother trying to rear her children respectably when they all know that their father has no regard for either decency or law.

A family trying to live down a scandal that sent the oldest daughter to suicide.

An investor whose profitable ventures have inflated his pride and made him careless with others' trust.

A physician under pressure to write narcotics prescriptions for a patron to whom he is financially obligated.

A trusted employee who for months has been embezzling from his firm.

A high-school youth torn between the license brashly advocated by his school's fraternity and the standards for which he has stood as officer in his church youth group.

A deacon enamored of the new office girl and beginning to play the fool.

A merchant seeing his little business, the work of half a lifetime, now declining under terrific competition from chain stores which he cannot possibly meet.

A social aspirant in whose heart envy and ambition have joined forces and are running wild.

An elder for whom religion has gradually lost its vitality and significance and has degenerated into mere formality.

A teacher who has devoted a quarter of a century in dedicated service to the community becoming disillusioned because public education is made a political pawn.

O God, bring Your healing and salvation to these we implore, through Jesus Christ. Amen.[25]

8

By whatever name we call You, by whatever mental image we think of You, grant, our God, that every soul here may find and be found.

Speak to us through the greatness of the universe which You have made our palace. Speak to us through beauty that lures us from the ugliness of life. Speak to us through the tragedy of war and human cries of despair that we may be moved with compassion and compelled to help the victims. Speak to us through Jesus Christ that we might be rescued from futile, aimless, selfish existence and be servants of Your purposes.

Father of Mercy, forgive us for our tendency to hear only what we want to hear, for the barriers we erect to keep us from exposure, for prejudgments that close the mind and lead to self-righteousness. Prick our consciences in some way through the wrongs which surround us. Stir us up to holy indignation and use us to take away whatever hinders Your kingdom of peace, plenty and harmony.

O Lord, there are among us griefs to be comforted, anxieties to be relieved, temptations to be fought, losses to be carried. Grant us the sincerity, surrender and unselfishness to say, "Here am I, Lord, use me." Amen.

9

Dear God:

We go out into a night that is growing dark,
But in the sky are countless stars.
Give us light.

We live at the edge of ghettos that are bleak.
But in them are children playing and laughing.
Give us hope.

The spirit of the poor seems gravely broken,
Yet, now they march upon the treasury of the earth.
Give us courage.

Young men are bleeding and dying in the East;
Still, we give thanks for dialogue in the West.
Give us peace.

The old structures bind us like Gulliver
While students of the world demand change.
Give us wisdom.

All things once so strong and sure seem to be passing,
And, behold new things everywhere!
Give us faith.

Tonight, O God, we celebrate
A great mystery,
For a sign of Thy grace has marked this place,
And Your promise like a rainbow
Is seen among us.[26]

10

Lord God, some of us have not come to this sanctuary very often. We are reluctant to come to this quiet place because we are afraid of silence.

Oh, we do not mind it as long as there is something to absorb our thoughts—music to listen to; someone moving to catch our glance; something to watch; something going on. We like activity. It's the silences we can't stand.

Whenever there is silence we get uncomfortable, embarrassed, restless. Whenever there is silence, we remember our transgressions, how we have offended You, ignored You, pushed You out; how we have abused others, even those we care most for, by our mean dispositions, gossipy natures, cruel attitudes, selfish absorption, withholding of praise and concern.

O God, I see now my past rising up before my eyes. I hear those I have offended speaking to me; I feel hot tears on my cold flesh. O God, through the silence speak Your forgiveness, that I might forgive myself. Cleanse me, O Lord.

Whenever we are silent, O Lord, by night or by day, we hear humanity's cries—cries of swollen-bellied children begging for food; of a hospital patient's agonizing groans calling, "Somebody help me!" We hear, too, the voices of friends growing old, incoherent, out of their heads; cries from broken hearts, broken homes; cries from crosses of sacrificial love.

If I am silent now, I can hear them. Disturb my complacency that I may care. Having cared, that I will be compelled to go from this place and become a channel of Your compassion and love.

It is in the silences that You speak to us in so many ways besides words, if we but listen with our hearts. Help me now to be still and to hear Your still, small voice, and to know that You are God. Amen.

11

Great God our Father, in whose wonderful image we have been created; we thank You for this gift. When we are tempted to think disparagingly of ourselves or of others, remind us of our relationship with You lest we forget that You made us but a little lower than Yourself.

Gracious Father, we confess that we have judged others' worth too much by superficial differences, like clothing, color of skin and physical characteristics. Remind us now, even as we stop at traffic lights and meet people on the sidewalks, that they are Yours no less than we are, and are precious to You. Remind us when the telephone rings, as we lift the receiver, a child of Yours will speak to us.

Help us, then, to have greater respect, reverence and kindness, likened unto Jesus.

As we pray, our Father, our hearts are heavy, for there are those we know and love involved in war, and those that we do not know, someone loves. We pray for them. We pray for their safety. We pray for their lives and the careers and families they hope to have when their work is done. May the marvels of modern medicine and surgery do their work in sustaining the lives of many injured men and women.

O God, prevail over the minds and hearts of all the nations involved in war. Grant their leaders insight into Your will; create in them a desire for peace and mercy and justice.

Support the world mission of the church, that more and more the causes of war—poverty, greed and frustration—may be eliminated and the climate of understanding may be created.

With longing in our hearts, we pray in the spirit of Jesus Christ. Amen.

12

Lord, let us do our work each day, and if the darkened hours of despair overcome us, may we not forget the strength that accompanied us in the desolation of other times. May we still remember the bright hours that found us walking over the silent hills of childhood or dreaming on the margin of the quiet river when the light glowed within us, and we promised our early

God to have courage amid the tempests of the changing years. Spare us from bitterness and the sharp passions of unguarded moments. May we not forget that poverty and riches are of the same spirit. Though the world knows us not, may our thoughts and actions be such as shall keep us friendly with ourselves.

Lift our eyes from the earth and let us not forget the uses of the stars. Forbid that we should judge others lest we condemn ourselves. Let us not follow the clamor of the world but walk calmly in Your path. Give us a few friends who would love us for what we are.

And though age and infirmity overtake us and we come not within the sight of the castle of our dreams, teach us still to be thankful for life and time's golden memories that are good and sweet and may the evening twilight find us gentle still, and keep ever burning before our vagrant steps the kindly light of hope. Amen.

13

Lord, it's sure nice to be here in this air-conditioned room, with cushioned pews, carpeted floors, beautiful windows and fine amplifying system, and a real pipe organ with fifty-six ranks. Most of us have come here from handsome, two-bathroom homes with modern appliances. We came in the second car, which has air conditioning too. Life has been good to us—better than we deserve—so we sing lustily, "Bless the Lord, Oh My Soul," for all is well.

Yet, we are uneasy because we know that within walking distance of this place are people that haven't eaten for a day, who are sweltering with 100 degree heat and have no fans or refrigerators. Some have dirt floors, no running water. Some have never owned a car. Young girls give themselves for a few dollars because they have no hope, no education, no skills. At least, they reason, this will buy something new and something to eat and someone to love.

God, we wish it were not true. We wish we didn't know—and we try not to. We wish we were only dreaming. We wish someone could prove that this is exaggeration. We wish we could say that these people themselves are totally to blame for their misery.

But down deep in the inner citadel of our being, where You speak to us, we know something is wrong and unjust, that something has caused this inequity. And we haven't really done our part to help cure it. Father God, You gave us all this world to be our home, capable of producing enough for everyone, where none need be deprived. You taught us to be brothers and sisters in Your family. It is not Your will that one of Your children be deprived while others live in luxury.

O God, disturb our comfortable, easy consciences and don't let us rest easy until we see and begin doing our part in relieving this predicament. Help us to know how to help others, how to right the wrongs, how to get better education, jobs and legislation for our unfortunate neighbors, and make us want to share our bounty so that we may be constructive yet keep us humble; generous yet not paternalistic; sympathetic yet not superior. Thus may the Kingdom come among the people where we serve and walk, to the end that more and more of Thy children may soon live healthily, happily and eternally. Amen.

14

Lord, I've just come upon this accident. Three college youths turning into a driveway, were hit from behind by a black man. It's an awful mess.

I don't know whose fault it was—it's hard to tell—but everyone's blaming the black. One of the youths right now is cursing him up and down. Another father is telling the police that the black was drunk and "how it really happened."

The police have searched the black man and made him "walk the line." He was chagrined, humiliated before the large gathered crowd. Everyone assumes the kids are innocent and the black guilty. And I guess the police will too, because he has no driver's license. He just bought the "old Cadillac yesterday." He'll pay for it—in jail—because he had no insurance and no driver's license.

But Lord, it *might not* have been his fault. The youth *might* have turned from the wrong lane. The turn indicator *might* not have worked. Isn't a person still innocent until proved guilty?

Lord, help us to withhold our judgments until the facts are clear—lest we prejudice others, prejudge the innocent—and injustice occurs. Amen.

15

We recall that wise men came to worship Jesus. Grant us the simple trust of the truly wise. Help us to know it is not gullibility to believe; that it isn't childish shallow sentiment to observe Christmas; that it isn't anti-intellectual, illogical or a defiance of science to pray or accept the Incarnation event. Forgive us if we have given hospitality to these ideas or taught them.

Humble us before the mystery. Forgive our conceit, and make us teachable. How little we really know; help us not to live by our doubts but by that which we can accept. Give us the honesty to mistrust our doubts. Allow our doubts to stimulate us to mature and intelligent faith.

Lift our eyes today from low views and motives which lead to suspicion and arrogance and littleness of spirit. Give us the courage to make new resolves and to keep them. Help us to look for the good before we do the bad, and the light before the shadows.

So capture our devotion, that we will put our time, energy and money to work for You, that the profits may be seen in human betterment.

From the churches of the world and the avenues of Thy spirit send comfort to the lonely wherever they be; send good cheer into the hearts of the sad; may those who feel offended forgive, and those who offend, repent. Let the gentle thoughts of peace, freedom, patience and goodwill fill the winds of the earth until guns shall be melted into plows, and the rivers of justice shall swell everywhere in the world. Amen.

SPECIAL PRAYERS

FOR ATHLETIC HEROES

Today we want to pray for the athletic heroes. How they thrill us! We include the ones who can hit the home run that wins a tie game, the quarterback who can throw the winning touchdown pass with only seconds left to play, and the basketball wizard whose skillful shooting brings victory as the buzzer sounds.

Lord, we spectators go wild over their feats. Thousands pay big money to watch their performance. Newspapers banner their names and carry their pictures, the pros offer fabulous sums, TV brings them into nearly every living room. Autograph seekers of all ages crowd upon them. Many with ulterior motives strive to manipulate and use them.

God, it must be difficult for athletes to keep humility, so we pray that these idols of our age may not think of themselves more highly than they ought to think.

Make them know that those whose names are in the headlines carry heavy responsibility; that those who are worshiped, must be worthy of adulation. For the sake of those whom they influence, help all athletes to be clean in speech, pure in motive, self-controlled, unselfish in attitude and unashamedly committed to Christ and His church.

Thus, may they and those whom they influence be equipped for the noble task of living, in the purpose of Jesus Christ. Amen.

FOR SCHOOL TEACHERS, ADMINISTRATORS,
AND BOARD MEMBERS

Lord, these school teachers, administrators and school board members deserve help. God, they have gone through extreme difficulties with the rebellious students, the integration transition, the emotional upheaval of parents, the controversies in curriculum, the pressures of unions, the take-over of militants.

Grant them, O Lord, patient cool in face of the defiant and rude. Help the teachers to be authoritative by a thorough grasp of their subjects without the authority of the badge or stick. May their discipline be mature, consistent and demanding, exercised with love and fairness. May the teachers be supported by wise and courageous administrators; may the administrators be supported by knowledgeable and principled board members; may the school boards be supported by an informed constituency which knows the issues of the day, the values of balanced education, and provide adequately to meet the demands of a changing world. Thus, may the students learn that which is worth knowing, and love that worthy of their affections, for the health of our nation and world. Amen.

FOR PHYSICIANS AND NURSES

We are especially appreciative, Father of compassion and healing, of those who care for the sick and afflicted. Grant to the physicians, not only wisdom and skill to diagnose and prescribe with accuracy, but the warmth and compassion that will reflect Your love to encourage the healing process. Save them from being impersonal, cold and calculating. Diminish greed with unselfish service that loses self in love for persons. Sustain the physicians in health for their long and ever-demanding hours of work.

We take our hats off to the vigilant nurses who work in such close proximity to the ill, in all kinds of conditions and moods. Provide them with understanding, kindness, goodwill, patience and spiritual commitment.

May the medicines remove the obstacles to health that the marvelous recuperative powers may prevail and wholeness in body, mind and spirit may eventuate. Amen.

FOR TV NEWSMEN

Lord, it's a great responsibility to be the molder of public opinion; to have the job of deciding what happenings in our nation and around the world will be photographed as news before 25 million or more people. It is awesome power to give editorial commentary regarding policy, personalities, national and international programs. Who is worthy? Who is equal to the demands?

So, today we pray that those who have been selected to be TV newscasters may be humble and unprejudiced, yet wise enough to choose a balanced diet of mental nourishment for the viewing public. May they be humble enough to avoid arrogance. May they be respectful enough to give credence to other's opinions and appreciation for views contrary to their own; yet fair enough to present honestly all sides of issues, allowing the survival of the fittest to be determined in the market place of ideas. Forbid that they should blindly and one sidedly belittle duly elected officials of our land, and may they hold them in due honor, even when they are being critical. May they be courageous and fearless prophets of social and political righteousness, speaking in the spirit of love. May they be men of faith who see in the unfolding of history's panorama, the long arm of God, the Determiner of all destinies. Amen.

FOR THOSE STRIVING FOR A BETTER WORLD

O God, we pray your special blessings upon all people who are striving to make this a better world, especially:

For all who are working for purer and more just laws.

For all who are engaged in relieving poverty and poor housing conditions.

For all who are seeking to rescue the fallen, helpless and hopeless.

For all who strive to mediate between opposing nations and segments of people.

For all who are working towards healing the brokenness of the church.

For all who witness for Christ in far away lands.

O Lord, defeat all evil designs and selfish schemes, and give encouragement and progress to all people and programs of goodwill conceived in the spirit of Christ. Amen.

FOR USING LIFE'S CIRCUMSTANCES

Planner of human life and Provider of all provisions for our happiness and health, we are grateful for the night to rest and the day to serve.

In all our circumstances, let us use disappointments as material for patience, success as material for thankfulness, suspense as material for perseverance, danger as material for courage, praise as material for humility, pleasure as material for temperance, pain as material for endurance.

Thus, may we be equal to the challenging opportunities of the day. Amen.

FOR PERSONS IN DIFFICULTY

Jesus, our Master, whose heart was moved with compassion toward the weak and oppressed, and who was more willing to serve than to be served; we pray for all conditions of people; for those lacking food, shelter or clothing; for the sick and all who are wasting away by disease; for the blind, deaf and lame; for prisoners; for those oppressed by injustice; for those who have lost their way in society; for the corrupted and morally fallen;

for the lonely and depressed; for the worried and anxious; for all living faithfully in obscurity; for those fighting bravely in unpopular wars or causes; for all who are serving diligently and dependably; for those who stand in the valley of decision; for those who are suffering the consequences of misdeeds repented of; for all family circles broken by death; for those faced by tasks too great for their powers.

Let the power of Jesus' spirit be strong within us, and those for whom we pray. Amen.

FOR WORKERS FOR RIGHTEOUSNESS

We pray for those who are engaged in settling affairs between peoples, that they may see all sides of issues and be led to the position that will reconcile.

We pray for all who write what others read, speak what others hear and mold public opinion in our time, that they may be responsible, knowledgeable, humble and led by truth.

We pray for those who are faced in making decisions with far-reaching consequences, that they may have insight to see the end from the beginning, and wisdom to choose right.

We pray for the unemployed whose poverty and idleness breeds corruption, that they may find useful work to direct their energies and provide for their needs. Amen.

FOR THE PROPHETIC MINORITY

O God, make us aware of the value of the dedicated minority which is radical, unpopular and disturbing, but so often idealistic and prophetic. However much we dislike their stubborn insistency, grant us the objectivity to listen to what they say. They may be a challenge to the lethargic status quo. They may be the wedge which alone can penetrate the entrenched and accepted evils. It must take courage to stand in such a dangerous, vulnerable position, but we need the prophetic minority lest we assume our society synonymous with your Kingdom. Save the minority from the insincere, selfish, haughty and publicity-minded. Help our leaders not to overly react until all challenges are silenced by the power of force and jail.

We remember long ago three men who died on Calvary—two because they were too bad; One because He was too good. Two were killed because they were below the level of society; One because He was above, disturbing and challenging the status quo. The gullible public crucified not only their sinners but also their Saviour. Forbid that we should do as they did. Amen.

FOR THOSE BEYOND HEALING

God of Compassion, we pray for those who seem beyond healing, for whom the skills of man can do nothing more, who must await the end. Even at such a time, grant them the serenity which is certain that nothing in life or in death, in time or eternity, can separate them from Your love.

Bless with the control and steadying power of faith, those who are nervous, those who worry so are distraught, those who find it difficult to cope with the inevitable. Grant to them gratitude for the gift of existence and the inward resources of faith to meet triumphantly every circumstance. Amen.

LITANIES

LITANY OF PRAYER

CHOIR (*in song*)   Our Father, who art in heaven.
LEADER   You are the ground of our being, the soil from which personality has emerged, and truth, love and justice blossomed.
RESPONSE   Hallowed be Thy name!

LEADER   We speak reverently Your name and humble ourselves in appreciation, admiration, and dependence.

RESPONSE   Thy kingdom come, Thy will be done on earth.

LEADER   How long, O God, how long? Above all our selfish goals and aspirations, help us to yearn and dream, pray and work for brotherhood among men. Amid the disorder, violence, and division, hasten the day, O Lord, through sensitive servants.

RESPONSE   Give us this day, our daily bread.

LEADER   Not for tomorrow and its needs, but for this day's responsibilities, provide us wisdom and strength, we pray, believing that if we fill this day with quality and live this day to its best, we can trust ample care of our future. Wherever and whatever be our condition, save us from worry.

RESPONSE   Forgive us our sins as we forgive those who sin against us.

LEADER   You have shown us your forgiveness of us in Christ. Even in our enmity, and in spite of our littleness, You have forgiven. Help us to not withhold mercy and love to those who abuse us, for in going the second mile, we find the barriers melting down and reconciliation effected. In the power of love is the hope for our fractured world.

RESPONSE   Lead us not into temptation, but deliver us from evil.

LEADER   Keep us from the influences which would degrade us, or cause us to be less than our best. O God, answer our Saviour's prayer through and in us, in the name and spirit of Jesus Christ.

CHOIR AND CONGREGATION (*in song*)   For Thine is the kingdom, and the power, and the glory forever. Amen.

LITANY ON THE ART OF GIVING

LEADER   In gratitude for God's gift of life to us we should share that gift with others. The art of giving encompasses many areas. It is an outgoing, overflowing way of life.

RESPONSE   Basically we give what we are. "The thoughts you think," wrote Maeterlinck, "will irradiate you as though you are a transparent vase."

LEADER   The gifts of things are never as precious as the gifts of thought.

RESPONSE   Emerson said it well: "Rings and jewels are not gifts, but apologies for gifts. The only true gift is a portion of thyself."

LEADER   We give of ourselves when we give gifts of the heart: love, kindness, joy, understanding, sympathy, tolerance, forgiveness.

RESPONSE   We give of ourselves when we give gifts of the mind: ideas, dreams, purposes, ideals, principles, plans, inventions, projects, poetry.

LEADER   We give ourselves when we give gifts of the spirit: prayer, vision, beauty, aspiration, peace, faith.

RESPONSE   We give of ourselves when we give the gift of time; when we are minute builders of more abundant living for others.

LEADER   We give of ourselves when we give the gift of words: encouragement, inspiration, guidance.

RESPONSE   We should give of ourselves with the radiant warmth of sunshine and the glow of the open fire.

LEADER   We should give our community a good man.

RESPONSE   We should give our home a devoted husband and father.

LEADER   We should give our country a loyal citizen.

RESPONSE   We should give our world a lift toward "that one faroff divine event toward which all creation moves."

LEADER   The finest gift a man can give to his age and time is the gift of a constructive and creative life.[27]

LITANY OF THE BEATITUDES

LEADER   Blessed are the poor in spirit.

RESPONSE   I am open and receptive to the inflow and the outpouring of all there is in God.

LEADER   Blessed are they that mourn.

RESPONSE I am grateful for the challenges that lead me beyond my extremity to God's opportunity.

LEADER Blessed are the meek.

RESPONSE I am in tune with God [harnessed for God's purposes]. That which is God-inspired and God-directed shall prevail.

LEADER Blessed are they that hunger and thirst after righteousness.

RESPONSE I seek [for righteousness] with all my mind and heart, and I shall find.

LEADER Blessed are the merciful.

RESPONSE I keep my thoughts centered upon only those things that I want to see manifest in my life.

LEADER Blessed are the pure in heart.

RESPONSE I see the world, not as it is, but as I am when I am in spiritual unity with God.

LEADER Blessed are the peacemakers.

RESPONSE I am a child of God and I act like one. I am a radiating center of peace and love. [In my quest for truth I press on past my humanity to a deepening awareness and an increasing releasement of my potential divinity.] [28]

LITANY OF FORGIVENESS

LEADER

Today upon a bus, I saw a lovely maid with golden hair;
I envied her—she seemed so gay—and wished I were as
     fair.
When suddenly she arose to leave, I saw her hobble down
     the aisle;
She had one foot and wore a crutch, but as she passed, a
     smile.

RESPONSE

O God, forgive me when I whine;
I have two feet—the world is mine!

LEADER

And then I stopped to buy some sweets.
The lad who sold them had such charm.
I talked with him—he said to me,
"It's nice to talk with folks like you.
You see," he said, "I'm blind."

RESPONSE

O God, forgive me when I whine;
I have two eyes—the world is mine!

LEADER

And walking down the street,
I saw a child with eyes of blue.
He stood and watched the others play;
It seemed he knew not what to do.
I stopped a moment, then I said,
"Why don't you join the others, dear?"
He looked ahead without a word,
And then I knew, he could not hear.

RESPONSE

O God, forgive me when I whine;
I have two ears—the world is mine!

LEADER

With feet to take me where I'd go,
With eyes to see the sunset's glow,
With ears to hear what I would know,

RESPONSE

O God, forgive me when I whine;
I'm blessed, indeed! The world is mine!

LITANY OF SERVICE

LEADER   We pause just now to think about those who are sick,
hungry, deeply troubled, unemployed, stranded, poor, lonely,
mentally confused, and burdened in other ways.

RESPONSE   We remember One who had compassion upon the sorrowful, wept with the lonely, healed the sick, took time to assist those in trouble, and stirred people up to good works. May we, His followers, not be content to "sit out" our Christian lives on cushioned pews.

LEADER   In the light of our Christian calling to servanthood, we would evaluate our jobs and opportunities, and the ways to help the refugee, the unemployed, the alcoholic, the orphan, the unmarried mother, the victims of tragedies and the physically handicapped.

RESPONSE   O God, make us like our Master—a servant to neighbors, shepherd to the straying, comforter of the sorrowful, protector of the weak and helpless.

LEADER   May we not be content only to meet physical or mental needs. Also help us to minister to the deep, unuttered yearnings of people's souls.

RESPONSE   Thus, O Lord, may we demonstrate Your love in our serving, so that those we serve may sense a purpose that makes life significant and the God of life, good.

LITANY OF STEWARDSHIP

LEADER   Maker of Heaven and Earth, by whose design we have come to life; in whose image we have been cast, by whose kind providence opportunity and responsibility have come our way.

RESPONSE   Help us to know we are accountable to You, the owner of all things seen and unseen.

LEADER   We thank You for the allotment of time which is the essence of our life and without which we could do nothing.

RESPONSE   Help us to use all our hours in ways that will please You.

LEADER   We thank You for the ability to learn and to do many things.

RESPONSE   Help us to develop and use our varied skills in a significant way for advancing Your Kingdom of right.

LEADER   We thank You for money and for what can be accomplished with it.

RESPONSE   Grant that all our earning and spending, all our investing and giving may be acceptable to You and will honor Your ownership.

LEADER   We thank You for the natural resources of the earth.

RESPONSE   Grant that we may use responsibly the soil, air and water so that future generations may not have polluted and depleted resources.

LEADER   We thank You for freedom.

RESPONSE   Help us to use our freedom to be our best, to support worthy purposes and to influence others to Christian behavior and commitment.

LEADER   We thank You for health of body and mind.

RESPONSE   Grant that we may avoid all habits and abuses that unnecessarily reduce our physical and spiritual well-being.

LEADER   We thank You for the good news in Jesus Christ that has changed forever the human outlook and has given us hope.

RESPONSE   Grant that we may take it seriously in our own lives, and be under compulsion to communicate it to others, here and everywhere.

LEADER   In the name of Jesus, we pray.

RESPONSE   Amen.

LITANY FOR HUNGER FOR MEANING

LEADER   Growing deeply inside of us, despite the achievements of our technology, is a hunger that will not let us go:

RESPONSE   O Lord, we yearn for some clue to the real significance of our lives.

LEADER   The apprehension haunts us that life at its core makes little sense. Deeper than the anxiety of guilt or death is our anxiety of emptiness and meaninglessness.

RESPONSE   We hunger for meaning and purpose, O Lord.

LEADER   Against the backdrop of Jesus' life and mission of service, may we see purpose for our own.

RESPONSE   Assuage our thirst with a knowledge of Your plan, O God, that we may rejoice in the life of opportunity which is ours.

ALL   O God, You have made us for Yourself. We are restless and frustrated until we find significant meaning in Your business. Satisfy our hungers now, through Jesus Christ. Amen.

LITANY OF CONFESSION

LEADER   O Divine Father, Your mercy ever awaits those who return unto You in true lowliness and contrition of heart. We come to You now ashamed and burdened with memories of things undone that should have been done, and things done that should not have been done.

RESPONSE   For deceitful hearts and defiling thoughts; for barbed words spoken deliberately, and thoughtless words spoken hastily; for envious prying eyes; for ears that rejoice in iniquity but not in truth; for greedy hands and loitering feet; for opportunities lost and blessings thanklessly received,

UNISON   Have mercy upon us, O God.

LITANY OF DEPENDENCE

LEADER   We acknowledge that however wise, or saintly, or rich we may be, we cannot live without daily food.

RESPONSE   O God, provide us this day our daily bread.

LEADER   We thirst for water and hunger for food because we are not bodiless beings, but men and women of nature, kin to the animal, with physical hunger.

RESPONSE   We acknowledge our dependence upon You, God, who has provided a world that will grow food and created our organs to assimilate it in marvelous ways.

LEADER   In a nation whose industry and farms and factories have achieved the highest standard of production and wealth of any time, we find it difficult to feel dependent upon God, and often feel it superfluous and outmoded to give thanks.

RESPONSE   Reveal to us the illusion of our self-sufficiency. Help us to know the limits of human knowledge and ability, and to realize in some measure how utter is our dependence upon all who assist in the food production and packaging and for the Divine Wisdom and Eternal Energizer of all.

ALL   Blessed be God, the Maker and Giver of all we see and all that we do not.

PRAYER   O God upon whom we ultimately depend for all things; forgive us for playing as if we were God and for failing to acknowledge our total need of You for daily existence. Amen.

LITANY OF PRAYER

LEADER   Jesus said, ". . . when you pray, go into your room . . . and pray to your Father who is in secret; and your Father who sees in secret will reward you" (Matthew 6:6).

RESPONSE   O God, make Your presence real and personal to us now, as we withdraw in reverent conversation with You.

LEADER   Jesus said, "Ask, and it will be given you; seek, and you will find; knock, and it will be opened to you" (7:7).

RESPONSE   O God, grant us persistence in our praying.

LEADER   Jesus said, "Do not fear, only believe" (Luke 8:50).

RESPONSE   O God, remove our doubts and dispel our fears with faith.

LEADER   Jesus said, "Watch and pray, that you may not enter into temptation" (Mark 14:38).

RESPONSE   O God, use our prayers to redirect and to restrain us.

LEADER   Jesus said, ". . . seek first his kingdom and his righteousness" (Matthew 6:33).

RESPONSE   O God, save us from selfish pleas and make your kingdom the content of our prayers.

LEADER   Jesus said, "Love your enemies, and pray for those who persecute you" (6:44).

RESPONSE   O God, incline our hearts to active concern and good-will for those we do not understand and may our prayers soften the resentment and bridge the gaps.

LEADER   Jesus said, "Pray then like this:
Our Father in heaven:
Holy be your Name,
Your kingdom come,
Your will be done,
    on earth as in heaven.
Give us today our daily bread,
Forgive us our sins,
    as we forgive those who sin against us.
Save us in the time of trial,
    and deliver us from evil.
For yours is the kingdom, the power, and
    the glory forever. Amen" (Paraphrased from Matthew 6:9–13).

COMMUNION MEDITATIONS

NOT BY BREAD ALONE

Man does not live by bread alone, but by beauty and harmony, truth and goodness, work and recreation, affection and friendship, aspiration and worship.

Not by bread alone, but by the splendor of the firmament at night, the glory of the heavens at dawn, the blending of colors at sunset, the loveliness of magnolia trees, the magnificence of mountains.

Not by bread alone, but by the majesty of ocean breakers, the shimmer of moonlight on a calm lake, the flashing silver of a mountain torrent, the exquisite patterns of snow crystals, the creations of artists.

Not by bread alone, but by the sweet song of a mockingbird, the rustle of the wind in the trees, the magic of a violin, the sublimity of a softly lighted cathedral.

Not by bread alone, but by the fragrance of roses, the scent of orange blossoms, the smell of new-mown hay, the clasp of a friend's hand, the tenderness of a mother's kiss.

Not by bread alone, but by the lyrics of poets, the wisdom of sages, the holiness of saints, the biographies of great souls.

Not by bread alone, but by comradeship and high adventure, seeking and finding, serving and sharing, loving and being loved.

Man does not live by bread alone, but by being faithful in prayer, responding to the guidance of the Holy Spirit, finding and doing the loving will of God now and eternally.

WHY I COME TO THE LORD'S TABLE

I come not because I am worthy, not for any righteousness of mine. For I have sinned and fallen short of what, by God's help, I might have been.

But, I come because Christ bids me come. It is His table. And He invites me.

I come because it is a memorial to Him, as oft it is done in remembrance of Him. And when I remember Him—His life, His sufferings and death, I find myself humbling myself in His presence and bowing in worship.

I come, because here is portrayed Christian self-denial, and I am taught very forcibly the virtue of sacrifice on behalf of another which has salvation in it.

I come, because here I have the opportunity to acknowledge my unworthiness and to make a new start.

I come, because here I find comfort and peace.

I come, because here I find hope.

I come, because I rise from this place with new strength, courage and power to live for Him who died for me.

BEFORE JESUS

BEFORE JESUS the cross was a cruel instrument of man's cruelty. Since Jesus it has become the most revered symbol in the world.

BEFORE JESUS the cross was the method by which hatred and jealousy and enmity eliminated those they opposed. Since Jesus, it has become the method by which sacrificial, vicarious compassion and love born of God reconciles those in enmity.

BEFORE JESUS men bowed down before the cross cringing, fearful, defeated, hopeless. Since Jesus they rise with new faith, hope and love—empowered to face life and death.

ON THE CROSS Jesus' body was broken and his life blood drained—an investment in nothing less than our redemption.

OFFERTORY MEDITATIONS AND PRAYERS

SEE THIS BILL?

Lord, you know this bill's history and its secrets. It has passed through many hands

—of persons who have knocked themselves out to possess it for a few hours;

—of persons who have sacrificed honor and conscience, to have through it a little pleasure, a little joy.

Oh, what stories this bill can tell from its long, silent journey: "I have purchased bread for the family table. I have bought corsages and gifts of affection for young lovers. I have paid for a wedding ceremony. I have brought laughter to the young, and joy to the elders. I have bought books to inform the mind of all ages. I have paid for medicines and physicians to save the sick. I have been given to clothe and feed the unfortunate. I have been given to honor God's ownership, and support the church's ministry.

"But also I have bought liquor that has debased human potential. I have produced movies unfit to be shown to children and have recorded indecent songs. I have paid for human blood, and broken the morals of adolescence. I have been used to print pornography and to purchase the body of a woman for a few minutes. I have paid for the weapons of crime and war."

Lord, I thank you for all the joy and life this bill has brought. I ask your forgiveness for all the evil it has made possible. I offer it now as a symbol of my gratitude, and my convictions, and dedicate it to your spiritual purposes as known in Jesus Christ.

WITH A LOVE-FILLED MIND

God bids me greet this day with a love-filled mind. How can I do this?

I will look for the good and beautiful to appreciate—which I usually take for granted in the busy rush of everyday; yet I will see in the unpleasant, opportunities for good.

I will be thankful for the sun for it warms the earth and makes things grow; yet I will love the rain for wiping away the dust of the earth and cleansing my spirit. I will love light for it illumines my way; yet I will appreciate the darkness for it shows me the stars. I will welcome happiness for it fills my moments with joy and laughter, yet I will accept sadness for it opens the soul. I will receive humbly life's rewards, yet I will face obstacles for they become life's challenges.

God bids me greet this day with a love-filled mind. How then will I speak? When I am tempted to criticize I will hold my tongue and not vocalize until I can think of something to commend. Always will I seek for actions to applaud; never will I dig for excuses to gossip. I will be generous to my enemies and they will more likely become my friends; I will encourage my friends and they shall become my brothers.

God bids me greet this day with a love-filled mind. How then will I act? I will appreciate all kinds of people, for each contains an image of God. I will love the young for the idealism they emanate; yet I will love the old for the wisdom of their experience. I will love the beautiful for they are often loved only for their beauty; yet I will love the ugly for the depth of soul they often achieve. I will appreciate the ambitious for they inspire me; yet I will love the failures for the lessons they teach. I will love the wealthy for they are often courted only for their money, so are lonely; yet I will love the poor for they are sad, depressed and need concerned friends. I will love those in high positions because the responsibilities of far-reaching decisions are burdensome; yet I will love the meek for they are divine.

God bids me greet this day with a love-filled mind. How then will I react to others? With love I will tear down the walls of suspicion and hate which they have built around their hearts, and in its place will I build a bridge so that my love may enter their souls. Just as love is a weapon to open the hearts of men, it is also a shield to blunt the arrows of hate and the spears of anger. Such love will protect me in the market place, and calm me in times of tension. With such love will I walk unencumbered among all stations of people, and the shadows that I cast will ever lengthen.

HOW BIG IS YOUR CHURCH?

"How big is your church?" one is often asked,
To aptly determine how it may be classed.
The answer depends on the standard of measure
And not on the whims that bring members pleasure.

The church is not rated by windows and spires,
But by what it believes and its worship inspires,
By what it expects and what it requires,
The concerns that burn on its altar fires.

Not alone do we measure by numbers and names
But by what a church gives and what it retains.
No church would we measure by buildings and walls,
But by its response to great needs and calls.

The church is as big as the world it claims,
As broad as its outreach, as great as its aims,
Each church is as big as its budgets for missions,
As profound as its sense of the Great Commission.

God looks at our hearts and not at our fashion,
At what we believe with conviction and passion.
Ourselves and our church we must always measure
By the sacrifice we make and not by our treasure.[29]

MORE MEDITATIONS

1

Through your offerings you witness for Christ in many ways.
Your dollars become your feet, your hands, your tongue. Others,
who are supported by our dollars, go in our behalf to serve for
Christ.

If you doubt the importance of the agencies which your church
supports, then try preparing one Sunday school lesson for each
age level in your church; try by yourself caring for hundreds

of aged citizens or homeless children; try recruiting youth for the ministry and organizing staff and supporting the colleges and seminaries for their training; try supporting home and world missionaries.

Your dollars added to others accomplish this and more.

2

The parents of a young man killed in the war gave their church a check for $200 as a memorial to his memory. When the presentation was made, another war mother whispered to her husband, "Let's give the same for our boy."

"What are you talking about?" asked the father. "Our boy didn't lose his life."

"That's just the point," replied the mother. "Let's give it because he was spared."

STEWARDSHIP PRAYER

3

We come now to give what we could use to buy something nice for ourselves. Perhaps we come to give what we really cannot afford to give. Yet, we feel compelled by the love of Christ who invested His very life blood. Take then our gifts from our hearts and bless them by the Spirit of Christ, that men and women may know Your love is alive, and find hope. Protect from temptation, all who handle these dedicated funds. Restrain greedy recipients. Hasten the day when Christ's spirit shall reign in the hearts of all men.

4

Lord, I remember you,
  your cross
  your love for me,
  your sacrifice.

I remember those persons who have sacrificed
  energy,
  ease,
  money,
  joy,
    for me.
Make me willing to spend myself
  for those whose lives are bound up with my own;
Lord, I remember you.[30]

5

Lord, let us share through attention given to others, Your loving concern for us. Let us adore in others the mystery of Your creative love. Let us in our unselfishness convey to others some degree of Your self-humbling sacrifice for us as seen in Jesus Christ. Amen.

6

When God made the earth, He could have finished it, but He didn't. Instead, He left it as raw material—to set man to thinking and experimenting and risking and adventuring and creating.

God gave us a world *unfinished* so that we might share in the joys and satisfactions of creation.

He left the oil in the rocks. He left the electricity in the clouds. He left the rivers unbridged, and the mountains untrailed. He left the forests unfelled and cities unbuilt. He left the laboratories unopened. He left the diamonds uncut. He left the music unsung, and the dramas unplayed. He left the poetry undreamed, and the stories untold.

And, best of all, He left to man the unfinished world of concern for children—the unfinished world that encompasses the disadvantaged, the physically handicapped, the retarded, the children of minority groups, and that great mass of children we call "average."

God gave man the challenge of raw materials, not the satisfaction of perfect, finished things. And therein we find our supreme challenge.

We have a world to build.

When the late Dr. Kagawa, the famous Japanese Christian, visited the churches of America, some years ago, he said, "What we need is fire." When interrogated about what was meant by *fire*, the answer came, "Fire is the leaven of discontent that somebody puts in to make life better than it was the day before. You must foster within the church the leaven of discontent which is fire. Once it is kindled, nothing else matters—no organization —nothing. And unless it is kindled, nothing matters."

THE AGONY OF GOD

I listen to the agony of God—
  I who am fed,
  Who never yet went hungry for a day.
  I see the dead—
  The children starved for lack of bread—
  I see, and try to pray.

I listen to the agony of God—
  I who am warm,
  Who never yet have lacked a sheltering home.
  In dull alarm
  The dispossessed of hut and farm,
  Aimless and "transient" roam.

I listen to the agony of God—
  I who am strong,
  With health, and love, and laughter in my soul.
  I see a throng
  Of stunted children reared in wrong,
  And wish to make them whole.

I listen to the agony of God—
  But know full well
  That not until I share their bitter cry—
  Earth's pain and hell—
  Can God within my spirit dwell
  To bring His Kingdom nigh.[31]

BENEDICTIONS

1

Spirit of Jesus, present now within our hearts; we are thankful for the sacraments of which we have eaten and drunk to remember our Lord's death and taste His living presence; for all the earthly symbols by which unseen realities have a firmer hold upon our souls; for the music which has inspired us, the fellowship that has encouraged us and the interior peace that has quieted us. Grant, our Heavenly Father, that the spiritual refreshment we have experienced may strengthen us in our Christian witness to honor Christ's love and spirit. Amen.

2

Here we have drunk from the fountain for inward strength. Here we have found a light to enlighten our road. Here we have felt a purifying wind to blow through all our businesses and pleasures.

Therefore, O God, enable us as we go from this place to be strong in our Christian commitment of service and love, in Christ's spirit. Amen.

3

Divine Parent, let Thy highest blessings rest upon each of us and upon Your church everywhere, now and forever more. Amen.

4

MINISTER   May the peace of God dwell in your hearts.
CHOIR (*in unison*)   Forever.
PERSON IN ONE SECTION   Forever.
ANOTHER PERSON IN ANOTHER SECTION   Forever.
ANOTHER PERSON IN ANOTHER SECTION   Forever.
MINISTER   So may it be.

5

May the Lord bless you and keep you—**OUT THERE.**
May the Lord make His face to shine upon you and be gracious to you—**OUT THERE.**
May the Lord lift up the light of His countenance and give you peace—**OUT THERE.**

6

MINISTER   The Lord bless you, everyone.
CONGREGATION (*shouting*)   **AMEN!**
MINISTER   The Lord is with you, everyone.
CONGREGATION (*whispering*)   Amen.
MINISTER   The Lord loves you, everyone.
CONGREGATION (*singing regular three-fold Amen tune*)   Amen, Amen, Amen.

7

Go now remembering what we have done here. Go, remembering what God has done here. You are a forgiven people, eternally loved, charged to be obedient and responsible where you are. We go into the world to be God's people. May His peace and joy be with you. Amen.

8

God sends you from the gathered church, to be the scattered church let loose in a world that is resistant to Him. Into your varied occupations, may you make your world His world, a world that is "new in Christ." May God's spirit go and abide with you. Amen.

9

LEADER   May God's love give you confidence.

CHOIR   Amen.

LEADER   May God's truth give you direction.

CHOIR   Amen.

LEADER   May God's eternalness give you peace and hope this day and all your days.

CHOIR   Amen.

Section 3

SERMONS: SUCCESSFUL EXPERIMENTS

Sermons

Interviews

Choral Readings

Dramatic Presentations

DIALOGICAL BIBLICAL SERMON
Lost and Found

(*LUKE 15:11–32*)

YOUNGER Hello, Brother Edward, how have you been? It certainly is good to see you.

ELDER I heard that you'd come back. As a matter of fact, I heard the ruckus you and the others made most of the night!

YOUNGER We missed you at the party. Dad, some of our relatives, the servants—just about everyone was there. And we all had a good time; even I did.

ELDER What do you think would happen around here if we ran that kind of three-ring circus every night? Someone had to get to bed and be on hand to see that things got started on schedule today!

YOUNGER I suppose it was a bit of a circus: the giving of my new robe and ring, the fatted calf, the dancing and singing, and the rest; but it meant a great deal to me.

ELDER And that fatted calf also meant a great deal to me. You're going to have to be the one that goes to tell the priest at the temple that we don't have a fatted calf for the atonement sacrifice. It's explicitly required in the Law that there be one; you and Father should have remembered that.

YOUNGER Surely the priest will understand why Dad used it for the party. It isn't every day that a son finds his life as changed as mine has been.

ELDER Changed? Your money runs out, your women leave you, and you come running back with your tail between your legs like a sick dog!

159

YOUNGER I knew some people would look at it that way, but I had hoped you wouldn't be one of them. Why don't you try to understand, Edward?

ELDER What is there to understand? You were never really happy here at home with Father and me—always wanting to do different things; always having radical ideas. I knew you'd do it sometime—leave us to do your work for you and then go out and lose everything that was given to you.

YOUNGER I knew that you felt that way years ago, Edward. You had a way of making me feel guilty about what I did. But I know a little bit more about life now than I knew then. I know that a man can't be happy by just fulfilling the requirements of his conscience. There's more to a man than that—there's sensitivity and curiosity; there's a desire to feel that one's own initiative means something; there's a need to find oneself, to be free from the traditions and the expectations of the people around you.

ELDER What more do you know now that will help you back here—on our land and with the duties of the temple worship? It seems to me that you always wanted to be free from everything binding. Maybe you should have stayed at home, and learned to be free from your fleshly desires and need of adventure right here.

YOUNGER Maybe you're right. Maybe I could have found that freedom at home—but you certainly never did anything to help me along. You were always too busy to stop and talk about some of the things that bothered me. You never even took the time to find out if there was anything that bothered me. And instead of doing something helpful about the time and money that I wasted you only talked to Dad behind my back and dropped comments to the rabbis.

ELDER Seems to me you're getting awfully confused. What does being happy have to do with it? We have to have specific rules to follow each day. What else brings character, friends, and success? How else can we tell the good people from the bad? I've never said I was perfect, and I do have my ups and downs like everyone else, but it seems to me that I'm a lot better off right now than you are—with all your money gone, with a bad reputation, and with no real friends and a dissipated body. Yes, I guess that I am proud of the fact that I'm not you, that I've never given into sensuality. I'm proud that I stayed home!

YOUNGER Stayed home! Stayed home! You can't get off that same old track. But stayed home for what? You've built a life here, but what kind of life? A life built not on righteousness but on reputation; not on the generosity of the heart but on the sacrifices of the temple, not on a deep concern for people but on a coating of sociability. This isn't living, Edward. It just isn't living!

ELDER Well, the amazing thing about you is that you can come back home and let Father stay up half the night bribing you with riches to keep you home, and apparently have no guilt whatsoever. And now you're criticizing me! You act like you were gone only a few days. Have you forgotten already?

YOUNGER If I haven't, it's because you won't let me. If you felt about me the same as Dad does, you would have been sharing his grief, and been hoping for me to come back, as he did; you would have welcomed me, too, and been with us last night.

ELDER That's the fanciest evasion I ever heard—trying to say that you're righteous and that I'm guilty! You're only clouding the issue; the facts are clear to me. If Father were to weigh and compare your good deeds and moral achievements with mine, I'd come out way on top!

YOUNGER The simple but incredible fact that, in spite of my past, in spite of the requirements of the Law, even in spite of you and your attitude, Dad loves me and accepts me for what I've always been to him—his son. I've come home at last to stay. It is as if I were dead and now I'm alive; as if I were lost and now I've been found.

ELDER   It's much too easy. I just can't see it that way. . . .

YOUNGER   I know, Edward, but perhaps someday. . . .[32]

BIBLICAL CHARACTER INTERVIEW
A Visit to Bethlehem

(THE FOLLOWING CHARACTERS ARE INCLUDED IN THIS INTERVIEW: INTERVIEWER, MARY, JOSEPH, INNKEEPER, SHEPHERD, SIMEON, HEROD, MAGI.)

INTERVIEWER   Next (day of week) we will celebrate the birth of Jesus, whom we call the Christ. All around the far-flung earth there will be groups of people who remember Him with gratitude. Though it was two thousand years ago when the event of our Lord's birth occurred, let us set forth the Biblical circumstances and call forth the characters involved for their testimony as if it were a contemporary happening. Our first interview is with Mary, the one chosen to be Mother of Jesus. (*Enter Mary dressed in modern attire.*) Soon you are to become the mother of the Son of God. Mary, tell us your deeper thoughts when you learned you were to become the Mother of Jesus?

MARY
Why did he pick on me?
Why me?
Sure, I guess I'm special—but not that special.
Think of all the swingers he could have chosen.

But he picked me.
Maybe I'll be a celebrity now—a star.
My picture on *Photoplay?* A "Milestone" in *Time?*
It scares me sick.
And the part that scares me most is:
Why me? **WHY ME?**
It was so quick.
I was getting ready for dinner, fixing my hair.
(Joe was taking me out—"Someplace fancy," he said.)
Then the room got bright.
I thought it was the TV.
I heard a voice. Funny—I thought then it was the radio.

But now I know.
Now I am ready.
It's strange and mysterious, and it puzzles me;
But I accept it.
I won't ask any questions.

It burns inside me;
I'm happy, happy and excited.
And frightened.

INTERVIEWER   Bless you, Mary. Now, let us interview Joseph,
the one to whom Mary is engaged. (*Enter Joseph, dressed in
modern attire.*) Joseph, what were your thoughts when you
learned Mary was pregnant?

JOSEPH

It really shook me up
When she came and told me.
I just couldn't believe it.
It was just too much to swallow.
I mean—what if you had been in my shoes?
And yet she said it was true.

I was quiet for a long time.
We didn't have much to say—didn't know what to say.

I guess you know how I feel about her,
How much I love that girl.
She was in my every waking thought:
Mary, Mary, Mary!
It was always Mary.
And then a wedding had been set, plans made, everything.
And then **THIS** had happened.

For a long time I stayed away from her, thinking.
Then I went back, and asked her again,
Just once.
And she still said it was true.
So I believed her then:
Because I love her,
Because she said it.

INTERVIEWER   Thank you, Joseph. It would not be proper unless we heard directly from the Bethlehem Innkeeper, who has been so maligned. (*Enter Innkeeper.*) We want to hear from you, Mr. Innkeeper. You have been criticized much for crowding out the parents of Jesus, especially when she was obviously in labor. What is your defense?

INNKEEPER

I'm not really a bad guy:
I'm just tryin' to get by, doin' the best I can.
What with a wife and six hungry kids
It ain't always easy.
So when the young fella and his wife come along
I tried to do what I could for them.
Naturally, I didn't have no room,
What with the traffic and weather and all.
But I seen she was fit to burst
With the young'n she was carryin'.
"You can use the shed," I told 'em.
Course I didn't charge them the goin' rate.
(I told you I wasn't a hard-fisted man.)

Still, the shed was better'n nothin',
So I let 'em have it cheap.
And that's where the baby come.

No, I ain't a tight man.
But I don't give nothin' away neither;
What with a wife and six kids I can't hardly afford to.
Charity starts at home—that's what folks say.
So I just did as good by 'em as I could,
Doin' my best.

INTERVIEWER We understand you better, Mr. Innkeeper. Now
the shepherds were a part of the Biblical record. Let's call one
of them to the mike. (*Enter one of the shepherds.*) Tell us, sir,
what do you make of this happening in which you have been
involved? What does it all mean?

THE SHEPHERD

What does it all mean?
Just what is it all supposed to mean? That's what puzzles me.
And why was I picked to see it happen?
How did I get mixed up in it?

All I've got is questions, it seems—no answers.
I take that back. I've got one answer, I guess.
I can tell you this: it really happened.
Saw it with my own eyes.

I believe it because I was there. I know it happened.
But I don't know how come.
I've got an idea, a hunch, maybe.
I think I know—maybe.
And that scares the wits out of me.
It scares me because I know it happened.

If it'd been you, then it'd be easy; I could laugh at you.
I wouldn't be mixed up in it, wouldn't have to think about it
But it happened to *me*.

And, since I can't say it didn't happen,
Since I saw it, and heard the singing and all,
Why, then I *have* to think about it,
And this scares me
Because I don't want to believe it,
And yet I have to.
Because I was there, and I know I'm not crazy.
Maybe it means what I think it means;
And that puts me right in the middle.

INTERVIEWER   What a rewarding experience! Now, Simeon, a priest at the Temple, was the presiding clergyman when Jesus was brought to the Temple for purification according to the ancient Jewish custom. This was a significant responsibility, especially when it involved one of such mystery. Let us visit with the clergyman, Simeon. (*Enter Simeon.*) Simeon, is there anything unusual about this particular event? Do you feel differently than usual about your responsibility?

SIMEON

At last it happened!
No wonder my hands shake!
I've waited all my life for this day.
God knows how many mornings I've awakened before dawn,
   thinking:
Maybe this will be the day.

Sometimes I've had bad moments.
But I've really never lost my faith. Never really.
Never really doubted that, someday, it would happen.
(Didn't He promise me? Isn't He a Man of His word?)
He said it would be, and I believe Him,
I kept my faith
Knowing He would keep His promise.
Today He did.
And you wonder why my hands shake?
Well, sir, I'll tell you.

I'm a "man of the cloth," so the saying goes,
And I'm well acquainted with responsibility.
Today I have been given responsibility greater than any man
has ever known.
I am to bless him!
Then I can rest.
He has kept His word.

INTERVIEWER We all envy you this privilege, Simeon, thank
you for sharing your anticipation. The "bad guy" in the episode,
you will recall, was bitter, jealous King Herod. Perhaps, we
have not heard his side of things. Let us arrange an interview
with him. (*Enter Herod.*) King Herod, when the astrologers
from the Far East came by to visit with you about their sur-
mise regarding a newborn king, why did you react with such
violence?

HEROD
Who did they think they were talking to?
One of them said, "We came to see a king. Not you."
NOT ME?
Who's boss here if I'm not, huh?
Me, that's who. Me—Herod!
I'm the king.

I'll give them credit for one thing; they had guts.
They stood right in front of men and dared to talk that way.
Man—I should have said the word right then.
I should have said the word. Just a word—that's all it'd take.
Then we'd see who was king here, wouldn't we?

But I fooled them. I played dumb, went along for the ride.
And they spilled the whole story to me.
Now I know about the "other king."
Ha! He's as good as dead. I've already taken care of that.
They'll get Him, and soon too.
I told them to—and I'm king.

And, as for those foreigners, with the big mouths,
They've served their usefulness to me. They're living on bor-
    rowed time.
I have plans for them.

Then we'll see who's king around here,
Won't we?

INTERVIEWER   Perhaps you'll meet your match, Excellency. The
three wise men who journeyed far in search of the newborn
king are well known to young and old. One of them is with us
tonight. Let us hear his account of that experience (*Enter the
Magi.*) Tell us, what did you expect to find when you followed
the bright star? How did you personally feel after making this
discovery?

THE MAGI

I'm not sure what it was we expected to find
When we got here.
All I know is that we had to come.
Someone said: Go down to the brow of the hill.
Once we got the sign we were like sleepwalkers
Driven by a will that ruled us day and night.

We checked out the legends, read the histories,
And talked about it a lot, making plans.
And then we just dropped everything
And came.
We had to come. Somehow, we knew we had to come and see.

We didn't know what to expect:
Anything but what we found.
And yet . . .
Yet, when we saw Him, we knew we had finished our journey.
He was the reason we had come.

We had seen a light—choose what symbolism you will.
We had seen the light, and had come like moths,
Drawn to the flame.

And, when we reached the light
We were not disappointed.
Then we knew why we had come.
We shall return as different men.
We believe!

INTERVIEWER   Thank all of you who tonight have shared with us
a common encounter. We will all visit Bethlehem this season,
at least in thought; perhaps as one of these characters. May
a sense of mystery, awe and wonder cause us to approach the
season in reverence and humility.[33]

MODERN PARABLE SERMON
God and Man in Love and Motion

(Scripture Reading: John 15:1–21)

They were starting on a journey—the leader and his people.
The leader was a little to the fore, with all his followers bunched
closely together and only slightly behind. The people knew that
the journey would be long. They understood that there would be
hardships. They realized that the trip would tire them in ways
that would give their strength severe tests. But they were not
afraid. They trusted their leader, and they had confidence in
themselves. They did not always understand their leader, but
they were convinced he would never have started the journey
if its faraway end would not bring them happiness beyond
measure and joy like a river. So they put from their minds the
thoughts of trials. They went forth with hearts lilting and spirits
singing.

It was not long, though, before the difficult days on the road started to take their toll. Some of the people began to grumble. Why had they ever started on this stupid trip, anyway, they wanted to know. Why had their leader not tried to discourage them, since he knew it would be so hard? Why did he not hurry up and get them to some place where they could be happy?

Those who complained started a slowdown of sorts. They lagged behind. Others found interesting sights along the side of the road and stopped to dally here and there. Some wandered too far off on a bypath and were troubled in finding their way back to the main road. The people were no longer close together. Rarely could they hear one another call for help or shout out encouragement. Each one began to feel quite lonely. Worse yet, they had gotten so far behind their leader and his son that they could hardly see them. Thus they did not even know most of the time whether they were traveling in the right direction. At last, they were no longer a people at all. There were simply isolated individuals, in single file, each one seeing nothing of any other person except the back of the one in front of him, and even that at a distance. And there was a great, wide gap between their leader and themselves—so much so, that it finally happened.

No one knows exactly how it came about. There was no precedent for it. But, then, the world does not always require prior experience, does it?

I suppose the easiest way to explain it is simply to say that the world was out of balance. Here were the leader and his son. Far behind them were all the people, rutted down and pulling back hard because they did not want to go any farther. After all, they were tired; and so, it just happened. It was no one's fault. It was one of those strange freaks of nature, a scientific phenomenon, that will probably never again occur. There was a rumble—a deep-down rumble—coming, it seemed, from the center of the earth itself; it was a rumble that grew so loud that you knew it would have to escape if it were ever to stop. And escape it did. It came right through the crust of the earth and went tumbling off into space in wave after wave, until it was gone. And when the people looked, where the rumble had been, there was a great rent in the earth, a jagged tear as far as the eye, or even the mind's eye, could see. It was so deep that no one knew if it had a bottom at all. It was so wide that they could barely see across it. Their journey seemed to be at an end.

But that great fissure in the surface of the earth had a strange effect on many of them. Some could not have cared less and just sat down to make the best they could of always being on this side of the huge crack and never seeing their leader again. But others were more determined than they had been before to complete the trip. They wanted to be with their leader when he finally reached the land of so much happiness. So they endeavored to cross the great divide.

On the other side, the leader and his son could see the people. The leader called to them, but they did not seem to hear him. They had even misconceived the purpose of the journey. He had explained carefully that he was taking them to new fields of service for the world, where their lives would be more difficult than they had ever been. They agreed to go, but it had been because they thought they would end up with special privileges for having been so willing to help.

Some of the people felt they heard their leader calling to them, telling them how they might cross over to him, but they were not quite sure, and they did not want to take a chance on doing what he had said if they were not certain he had actually said it. Some claimed that he was not over there anyway, that he had gone on to the land of happy times without them. Others even said that there was no fissure in the earth, that no other side existed, that there had never been a leader, that their side was all there was or ever had been, and that the only thing to do was to make it the land of gracious living and green, crabgrass lawns.

The people could not agree on anything, and they became more and more suspicious of one another.

Once more, on the other side, the leader was in despair. He

could not continue the trip without his people, for they were the purpose of the journey. Yet they would not or could not hear him when he called instructions to them on how they could cross the chasm.

Finally, he hit upon a plan—his son. He had always been like them. They had understood him because he was like them. If only he could go to them with instructions on how they could cross. It was so simple if they would only understand. They just had to put their arms together and run at the divide. If they did, the sheer weight of their numbers and the momentum of their motion would carry them across.

So his son, with some unique power for motion, jumped across the divide, reluctantly leaving his despairing father alone. He went to tell the people how to make the crossover.

He was not greeted, however, in the way he had anticipated. Some were glad to see him. Others, though, had grown rather happy on the subtracted side of the division. At least, they thought they were happy. They did not want to leave their homes or the schools in which they were taught that there was no other side and no divide. They did not want to abandon the monuments they had built to their long-lost leader. After all, they really did prefer the memorials to the real leader.

Worst of all was that business of putting their arms around each other and running at the chasm. There are some people (you know the kind I mean) whom civilized people just do *not* put their arms around! And how could they be sure their momentum would carry them across? They decided that stability was preferable to motion. So they told the son of the leader to get lost.

He would not; so—you know what had to happen. It was no one's fault but his own. After all, law and order had to be maintained. You could not have people running all over telling others nonsense about putting their arms around one another. That might lead to all sorts of immorality. So they hatched a plot from the cracked shell of a spilled and spoiled dream. They tried him before the unworldly activities committee, and found that he was very unworldly. Why, he went all over putting his arms around all sorts of people: people with long hair on their heads and faces, and people who used bad words, and soldiers, and people who worked in banks and businesses, and physicians, and students, and policemen, and even deans. So they took him, and they beat all his great strength out of him, and they threw him into the great divide.

But as he dropped through the heavy air, his person almost broken, he summoned one huge loving fist of strength, and he stretched his body from one side of the chasm to the other. In doing so, he made a bridge for them to cross, or perhaps it was a cross for them to bridge.

There are still those who claim that the other side is not there. There are those who say that there is no chasm. Some cannot see the crossing bridge. But others know that, if you put your arms around someone, especially someone you do not like, if you go to where the chasm is at the place where the world is torn asunder, and if you run at it hard—if you just get into love and motion—there is no telling where you might go.[34]

TELEVISION PROGRAM TAKE-OFF
Mission: Impossible?

Characters NARRATOR, JIM PHELPS, CHIEF, MARTHA, MOTHER OF MARTHA, RADIO ANNOUNCER, OFFICER, PRESIDENT SMITH, GIRL STUDENT, MEMBERS OF MISSION IMPOSSIBLE TEAM, FATHER, SON.
Scene *In a church equipped with a public address system.*
   (*This sermon method takes a popular* TV *program and utilizes the built-in interest and technique to communicate a*

Christian message. Loosely based upon the long-popular CBS-TV program Mission Impossible, *this is an attempt to communicate to both sides of the so-called generation gap. A bridge of love and understanding is offered as a necessary solution. The mission is carried out in a series of scenes which reveal contemporary points of tension. For the final word, the Mission Impossible team evaluates the results. Then from another tape behind the cross, up-dated words of Jesus are heard. Appropriate musical selections should be used between the scenes.*)

Scene I   *The Opening of the Service*

(PHELPS *enters sanctuary from rear entrance, proceeds to pulpit or lectern, hesitates for a moment, then carefully removes "hidden" tape recorder from behind pulpit or lectern. He then places it near microphone of PA system.*)

CHIEF (*on tape*)   Good morning, Mr. Phelps. Your mission today is the most important you have ever been sent on, Jim. And the most difficult. For, you see, your enemy is invisible—he cannot be seen. And yet he casts a shadow on all people. He is a force, a power that invades our lives and destroys relationships between people. Your Enemy divides parents from children, students from teachers, adults from youth, black from white, rich from poor, friend from friend. Your assignment, Jim, should you accept it, will be to try to reunite these divided persons, especially those who are on the opposite sides of the so-called generation gap. As always, should you or any of your staff be captured by the Enemy, the Chief will forgive you and set you free. But, should you fail in your mission, Jim, the world will self-destruct in **one hour.**

Scene II   *Accepting the Mission*

PHELPS   The Chief has sent us on one of the most difficult missions of our career—to try to bridge the gap that divides the generations. Almost everyone admits that a vast difference of thinking and acting separates the young from the old. But almost *no* one can tell us precisely what to do about it!

One of the most apparent differences between the older and younger generations is the way by which they communicate: the older generation relies almost exclusively upon words and rational logic. The younger generation, for better or for worse, communicates dramatically, visually, by means of symbols and symbolic actions, often exaggerated for greater effect. The younger generation relies heavily upon the emotions and the senses; they are far more concerned with feelings than with thoughts. And this is the basic problem: neither generation can hear what the other is saying, and there is no communication.

We of the Mission Impossible Team will attempt to portray in drama and words the problem facing all of us today. Perhaps as we see with our eyes, hear with our ears, and feel with our hearts, we will gain a new perspective on the problem. The pictures we paint will be stark and bold; the colors are meant to clash; the brush is applied with heavy strokes; the effect is not often pleasant. But our portraits are meant to provoke, not to please. And if our portraits also bring new meanings and new understanding to the viewer, then we shall have accomplished our mission.

Scene III *Dating*

PHELPS As young people mature, naturally they want to become individuals; they seek their own identity in life, and sometimes this search for identity leads to tension in the home. Sons argue with their fathers, daughters argue with their mothers, and tempers often wear thin.

MOTHER Is that you, Martha?

MARTHA Yes, Mom. (*Just entering the house.*)

MOTHER   Come into the kitchen, will you? I've been waiting up for you.

MARTHA (*in the room now*)   Oh, Mom, why did you wait up?

MOTHER   You know very well why I waited up! I don't like your friend Charlie and I never have. I've learned a few things about him from members of my Circle, and I just don't like . . .

MARTHA   Oh, Mom. Charlie's OK. Just because he wears his hair long is no reason not to like him.

MOTHER   It's not just his hair—it's his whole attitude. It's as if he didn't care for anyone in the whole world but himself.

MARTHA   Charlie is a nice, decent boy, and I don't like your talking about him that way!

MOTHER   And look at the time! You're a half-hour later than your father and I agreed to! Where did you go after that movie?

MARTHA   Oh, we stopped off for a coke, drove around for a while, then he brought me home. (*Exaggerated.*) Gee, I'm sorry I'm late!

MOTHER   Martha, your father and I talked this over tonight, and we've agreed: you are not to accept any more dates with this Charlie character. We don't like his looks or his attitude, and we're not at all pleased with your attitude, either!

MARTHA   Mother! You're not going out with him, I am! And I'm going out with him again no matter *what* you say!

NARRATOR   Martha loves her mother. And her mother loves Martha. And yet, in the midst of this love, there is anger and frustration and withdrawal. The lack of trust destroys the relationship that exists between them.

PHELPS   Love is such a vague and hard-to-define word. It refers to almost *any*thing these days so that the word is meaningless unless we can pin it down to a specific situation. Trust, however, is much more specific. Trust is one way in which love makes itself known in relationships between people. Had Martha and her mother trusted each other, we might have witnessed another scene.

MOTHER Is that you, Martha?

MARTHA Yes, Mom. (*Just entering the house.*)

MOTHER Come into the kitchen, will you? I've been waiting up for you.

MARTHA Oh, Mom. Whydja wait up?

MOTHER Well, for one thing, it's a half-hour beyond our agreed-upon hour.

MARTHA I'm sorry, Mom, but we lost track of time.

MOTHER Martha, your father and I are not at all happy with your going out with Charlie. He doesn't impress us very much, I must say.

MARTHA I know he wears his hair long, but a person is more than just his hair. He's a nice guy, really he is, and I wish you'd give him a chance.

MOTHER All right, dear. Why don't you invite Charlie over to our home for dinner some evening next week. We really ought to meet him. After all, you and Charlie have been dating fairly regularly this month!

MARTHA (*jokingly*) Don't marry us off yet, Mom. But that's a swell idea about the dinner and everything. That's great, Mom!

MOTHER But when we say, "Be in by eleven," you be in by eleven.

MARTHA OK, Mom. (*Smiling.*)

Scene IV *The Campus*

PHELPS One place where the mission seems most impossible is on the college campus. Young people look upon higher education no longer as a privilege of the rich but as a right of all. Many college students are extremely vocal in their objections to administration policy and campus regulations. Dissident students are exerting power against the draft, ROTC courses, government-sponsored research, especially in the area of chemical warfare, and against practically all of the traditional moral standards held by older generations. These radical students are exerting power **for** classes in Black Studies, in some cases even seeking a separate school for black students, **for** a liberalization of entrance requirements in order to allow a greater number of disadvantaged students an opportunity to earn a college degree, **for** a liberalization of campus regulations in the areas of drugs and sex, and **for** most of the things their own parents are **against.** This is why the mission seems so impossible.

ANNOUNCER   My name is Ted Wilson. I'm a staff reporter for radio station WSNY. This is the campus of a leading state university. My job? To tell it like it is. Pardon me, Officer. May I have a moment of your time?

OFFICER   Who are you? Oh, a radio reporter. Yeah, I've got a minute. Shoot.

ANNOUNCER   Uh . . . oh, yes. Will you tell our listening audience what the situation is right now?

OFFICER   Well, things have calmed down now. The tear gas got 'em out of the administration building real quick!

ANNOUNCER   Was anyone hurt?

OFFICER   A couple of girls were overcome by the tear gas; otherwise no one was hurt. We didn't have to use our nightsticks at all. Let me make this perfectly clear—there's no such thing as police brutality on our force! I want that understood! (*Poking nightstick into announcer's stomach.*)

ANNOUNCER   Y-yes sir! Er . . . Officer, do you know the nature of their complaints?

OFFICER   Sure! They're just like all those hippies. They want the university to bow down to **them** and let **them** run the place the way **they** want to, and let the students do anything, anytime and anyplace they want to. Immoral, that's what they are —immoral.

ANNOUNCER   Thank you, Officer. . . .
Oh, here's the university president, President Henry Smith. Sir, may we speak with you for a moment? I'm with radio station WSNY and I'd like. . . .

SMITH Yes, yes, but just for a moment . . . I've a meeting with the university trustees in fifteen minutes, and I don't want to keep them waiting.

ANNOUNCER Of course not. President Smith, could you tell us your view of what has happened on your campus during the past twenty-four hours?

SMITH It appears to me that an attempt is being made by a small group of militants to destroy the university and all it stands for. Now there may be some justification for their complaints, but to defy the law and order of this historic institution of learning—well, that's going too far. Whatever merits their cause may have, these students have overplayed their hand, and the response of the community and the board of trustees will negate any possible progress from now on. Now, if you'll excuse me . . . .

ANNOUNCER Yes, sir, and thank you . . . Now, if I can get my microphone over to the police barricade that is keeping the crowd of students contained on the quadrangle, I'll try to speak with one of the students. Say, Miss, will you speak about your cause for our listeners?

GIRL Of course!

ANNOUNCER Please tell us your side of what has happened.

GIRL Sure! We kinda think it's about time the administration of this school began to listen to the students who pay good money to come here, and give them a voice in running this campus. We've got a right to be heard!

ANNOUNCER What is it you want them to hear?

GIRL We demand a higher representation of black students on this campus! We demand new courses that mean something, and don't merely support the middle-class status quo! We demand to have teachers who are open and willing to think as well as talk! And we demand that those campus recruiters get off this campus. Now!

ANNOUNCER And if you don't get your demands, what then?

GIRL   Mister, you'll find out. Just keep your little microphone handy, and bring the guys with the TV cameras. Then you'll find out "what then."

ANNOUNCER   Well . . . uh . . . thank you for your cooperation. I'll remember what you've said. This is Ted Wilson speaking from strife-torn State U., returning you to WSNY, the Radio Voice of Pleasant Valley.

FIRST TEAM MEMBER   Conflict on campus. Armed rebellion within the walls of Old Ivy. Students rising up against administration. The long arm of the law reaching into the dormitory. Angry faces lining the sidewalks. Fear stalks the community. And, whether the trustees like it or not, the whole campus is going to pot.

SECOND TEAM MEMBER   Or is it? Are we being fair? Are we hearing so much that we're no longer listening?

THIRD TEAM MEMBER   And what about the quiet majority? They have a voice, too. Sure, they have gripes. And their arguments may have merit. They should be granted a hearing and not be turned off like an unpleasant TV commercial.

FIRST TEAM MEMBER   Much of what is happening today on campuses around the country is like the farmer who slammed the donkey on the head with a 2 by 4 not to punish it but just to get its attention. Sometimes we need just such demonstrations to get our attention. Well, now they've got it, and we'd better listen, even if we don't agree. Nothing whatsoever will be gained by overreacting. Nothing is ever solved by guns and tear gas. Violence only begets more violence, and we can never be sure who controls the trigger.

SECOND TEAM MEMBER   And so, mister policeman, keep your cool, and you'll contribute to the solution by not being a part of the problem.

THIRD TEAM MEMBER   And you, militant student, you who wave high the standard of love, you keep your cool, and don't sacrifice your cause on an altar of destruction. *Be* heard! And

then listen. If your cause is just, it will prevail; if not, be ready
to accept it.

FIRST TEAM MEMBER   And you, mister college president, you
keep your cool, too. You've got a thin tightrope to walk, and
you're being pulled one way by the students whom you love,
and the other way by the trustees and alumni whom you
respect. Walk straight. Stand erect. For yours is the task to
make the mission possible.

Scene V   *Father and Son and the Draft*

PHELPS   While it may appear to adults that young people haven't
a care in the world, this is frequently not the case. In fact it
can be shown that teen-agers do care—about the course of this
nation and the world, about social injustice and inequity, about
civil rights and human rights and about war. Especially the
boys. Most teen-age boys are resigned to the fact that, sooner
or later, they will be called up to active service. Most young
men accept the draft as inevitable, and respond affirmatively.
However, an increasing number of young men are not.

FATHER   Son, will you please check the mail? I'm expecting a
letter from my accountant.

SON   Sure, Dad. (*Looks through mail, finds draft notice.*) Huh?
Selective Service! (*Opens letter and reads.*) Oh, God, I've been
drafted!

FATHER   What's the matter, Son?

SON   Oh, nothing . . . just my draft notice.

FATHER   Let me see . . . um . . . next month, eh? Well, you
knew that sooner or later it would come.

SON   Yeah, I know. It's just . . . well . . . oh, nothing.

FATHER   What's the matter? You're not afraid, are you?

SON   Yeah. But it's more than that. I'm not sure I agree with
what's been going on over there. In fact, I've been thinking
seriously of becoming a conscientious objector.

FATHER   What? Now, listen here, young man! Your brother is fighting in Viet Nam; I fought in World War II, your grandfather fought in World War I, and **his** father fought with Teddy Roosevelt! Why, we have a tradition of fighting for our country in this family! No, sir! No one is gonna call any son of mine a slacker or a coward! I'll not stand for it!

NARRATOR   Another flare-up. Another explosion in the home. Another break in communications between father and son, at a moment when a father is needed most. Sure the boy is scared. Who wouldn't be? Sure his father is upset. What father wouldn't be? But the father is scared, too, although he's too proud to admit it. He has his doubts, too, and even though he supports the policy of the government patriotically, he is being torn by his love for his *son* and his love for his country. And he takes it out on his son in the form of anger and hostility.

PHELPS   How much more honest this scene would have been had understanding and trust been present in the relationship.

FATHER   Son, will you please check the mail? I'm expecting a letter from my accountant.
SON   Sure, Dad. (*Looks through mail; finds draft notice.*) Huh? Selective Service. (*Opens letter and reads.*) Oh, God, I've been drafted!
FATHER   What's the matter, Son?
SON   Dad, I've just received my draft notice.
FATHER   Let me see . . . um . . . next month, eh? Well, you knew that sooner or later it would come.
SON   Yeah, I know. It's just . . . well . . . oh, nothing.
FATHER   You're frightened, aren't you?
SON   Yeah. But it's more than that. I'm not sure I agree with what's going on over there.
FATHER   I think I know how you feel, son. I was drafted, too, remember. And I was scared, too. Nobody likes war. Nobody

wants to leave the comfort and security of home to fight in some lonely foxhole, praying each moment that the shelling will stop so you can get a few winks of sleep.

SON But that war was **different**, Dad. We were attacked then, and war was easily justified. But now, well . . . the situation is different. (*Pause.*) Dad, I've been seriously considering conscientious objection.

FATHER I see. (*Pause*) Well, you probably remember what our pastor said a few weeks back in his sermon on this subject. "A Christian," he said, "must obey the feelings of his own conscience, informed by an understanding of Scripture, and moved by the Spirit of God." And Son, as a Christian, you have a responsibility to obey this higher calling. But remember what else he said: "For the Christian to choose to bear arms and fight in what he considers a just war is as much a Christian decision as to choose **NOT** to bear arms and **NOT** to fight in what he considers an unjust war. Both alternatives are equally valid Christian decisions." That's why your brother is fighting in Viet Nam.

SON Yes, I know. In fact, I've thought a lot about that.

FATHER Good! Now, you know where I stand on this issue of Viet Nam: I feel that our country is **right** to be there, and I support our government's policy 100 percent! But I'll say this, too. You're my son. And I'll stand behind any thoughtful, intelligent and prayerful decision you make. Ok?

SON Ok, Dad. And thanks. (*Shaking hands and looking at each other.*)

Scene VI *Summary*

PHELPS The generation gap—student unrest, rebellion against all authority, dissatisfaction with traditional forms of American life—these are symptoms of a complex problem which underlies every one of them. Our mission was not to analyze the problem, but to deal with the situation we now face: anger, hostility, separation, alienation, misunderstanding, and fear . . .

We have tried to portray instead: reconciliation, restored relationships, love, understanding, and hope. Have we succeeded? Only time will tell.

Scene VII *Conclusion*

(*Phelps steps from pulpit and joins M.I. group behind him*)

FIRST TEAM MEMBER The hour's almost up, Jim.

SECOND TEAM MEMBER Remember what the Chief said, Jim: "If we fail in our mission, the world will self-destruct in one hour."

PHELPS I know, I know. I can't help wondering if we've succeeded or if we've failed. It's so hard to know. The mission may not be impossible, but it certainly isn't easy.

THIRD TEAM MEMBER We know that, Jim. But remember this; we're not alone on this mission. There are thousands upon thousands of people like you and me who have similar impossible missions.

FIRST TEAM MEMBER That's right. And some of them succeed, and some of them fail. But the point is to **try,** and to take the risk that you *might* fail. The Chief knows this, and He understands.

SECOND TEAM MEMBER Our mission, Jim, is to try to bring people back together again, to restore dialogue between opposing forces, to bring reconciliation to a world that is torn into rival factions. It's a big job, we know, but that's what we've been called to do.

PHELPS You're right, of course. But sometimes I get to wondering if the world would be better off if it did self-destruct in an hour.

THIRD TEAM MEMBER You'd better get the final message from the Chief, Jim. You know where it's hidden?

PHELPS Yes, I know. *Descends steps, takes tape recorder from behind cross on table, returns to pulpit, plays tape.*)

TAPE This is your assignment, Jim, for you and the whole staff: that you love one another as I have loved you. There is no greater love than this—that a man should sacrifice his very life for his friends. You **are** my friends if you do what I tell you to do. I call you friends, now, because I have told you everything that I have heard from the Chief. Remember, you didn't choose **me**, but I chose **you** and sent you out to fulfill your mission. And since it was I who sent you, just mention my name whenever you ask anything of the Chief, and he will give it to you. This is your assignment: to love one another. I give you peace, Jim. Don't get uptight. And don't be afraid.

PHELPS (*pausing to close the recorder, he then raises his hands in the appropriate gesture*) Peace! [35]

MASS MEDIA SERMON

For the creative, imaginative minister, it is possible to use several media in a single presentation. For example, Archie Turner, campus minister, Madison College, Harrisonburg, Virginia, has done so with a message entitled,

PEACE WITH THE EARTH: THE LAST CHANCE—NOW!
(A message on "Ecology And Man's Responsibility")

The presentation is highlighted by a slide sequence timed to keep pace with narration, music, statistics, and congregational response. He uses one 80 slide carousel tray in building the slide sequence.

The first section portrays in word and picture the process of Creation, using "The Creation," one of seven black sermons in verse found in *God's Trombones* by James Weldon Johnson. "The

Creation" has been set to music by Roy Wingwald, and is recorded by Fred Waring and his Pennsylvanians. (Fred Waring has made several recordings of "The Creation." Be sure to choose one where the black preacher uses full voice range and pitch.) During the playing of this recording, 23 slides of word pictures from nature are shown. One should use his own creativity with the selections (perhaps a NASA earth photo) concluding with one or more slides pointing to the arrival of man in the chronology of creation. Approximate time is 3 minutes, 35 seconds.

The second section is a "tell-it-like-it-is" part. For a quick transition from the closing lines of "The Creation," the verse from Genesis is injected, *"And the Lord God took the man and put him in the Garden of Eden to till it and keep it"* (Genesis 2:15). Immediately the song "Air" from the musical Hair is played which starts, "Welcome, Sulphur Dioxide . . . The Air Is Everywhere." During this 1 minute, 25 second record, ten slides showing urban, suburban, and rural pollution and local environmental decay are projected. Usually the city planner will have slides available—or shoot your own.

To further amplify the "tell-it-like-it-is" section, another slide sequence is shown giving an overview of pollution problems: pesticides, water pollution, oil spillage, air pollution, mismanagement of resources, garbage disposal, sound pollution, population congestion, etc. While these are shown, two narrators read antiphonally research statistics, while *beautiful* background music from Bach or Beethoven is played. 3 minutes, 40 seconds.

The final section is designed to show the concerns of ecology in the Christian perspective, and to get people to think through their personal responsibilities. The leader reads Jeremiah 2:7, 15. A poster slide entitled, "The Ravished Environment" is flashed on screen while this litany is read.

Litany for Ecological Reflection

LEADER   Forgive us, Father, for we know exactly what we have done.

PEOPLE We know what we have done, and we stand accused.

LEADER We have made Your garden of creation a wasteland.

PEOPLE Lord, You have trusted us with so much, and we have been careless.

LEADER We have broken the great rhythm of life; the balance of nature.

PEOPLE Lord, we're sorry.

LEADER We have poisoned the sources of life—the air, the water, the land.

PEOPLE Thank You for loving us in spite of what we have done.

LEADER You have made us to be stewards, caretakers, to live in peace and harmony with all life. We have become tyrants, madmen who strip the earth in lust for progress. Our monuments of junk and rubbish proclaim the grim irony of success.

PEOPLE Teach us to live in interdependency.

LEADER You have invited us to be free, to be responsible, to be loving in all our relationships. We have said, "No, we prefer death to life."

PEOPLE Lord, show us the meaning of Life Together.

LEADER Father, forgive us for destroying the created works of Your hand. Destruction is the work of our hand.

PEOPLE Teach us the joy of creation as we pick up the pieces of life.

Next the leader reads Psalm 51:17 (NEB) and Isaiah 61:1, 2, 4 (RSV). Then the anthem, "This Is My Father's World," arranged by Ralph Carmichael (on Word album *Glory Hallelujah*) is played after which Psalm 8 (NEB) is read in unison.

The concluding song is "This Land Is Your Land" by Woody Guthrie, sung by Peter, Paul and Mary. The congregation is invited to sing along and watch 15 slides of remaining natural resources flashed rapidly on the screen.

DISCUSSION FILMS

The short film as well as slides are dramatic and useful aids for the "teaching sermon."

In this day when visual aids are becoming a cultural medium by which youth's attention is caught, this neglected tool has possibilities for creative teaching, inspiration and discussion. This method obviously is limited in worship to the sanctuary which will lend itself to this possibility.

SELECTED SHORT DISCUSSION FILMS

(See *Discovery In Films* for longer list of films on contemporary problems, and most denominational visual departments and camera catalogs for inspirational religious films.)

PARABLE   In the context of a circus, *Parable* epitomizes the history of mankind and of an individual man. Seven main characters play the roles of virtue-vice personalities of contemporary man; into each character's life comes the principal character—the clown in white who symbolizes Jesus as a man of unselfish action. He challenges each character to grow and become selfless. He is accepted by some persons but rejected and killed by others.

Magnus, the symbol of self-centered man, is the key character. The anger vented upon the clown by the jealous tantrums of Magnus occasion a new self-examination, and a total conversion. He becomes "the man who dares to be different" which is the theme of the film.

It is excellent for discussion. The interpretations depend upon what Biblical understanding one brings to his viewing. This film, used in the Protestant and Orthodox Center of the 1964–65 New York World's Fair, is proclaimed as one of the most eloquent, thought-provoking, contemporary films ever produced. Indeed, it is a powerful sermon. (28 minutes, color, 16 mm)

From: Modern Sound Pictures Inc.
1410 Howard Street
Omaha, Nebraska 68102

PLACE IN THE SUN   Two animated characters in this film struggle with each other for a coveted piece of sunlight. The sunlight suddenly disappears, and the characters realize that only by their working together can the sun be made to return, which they do. Clever cartoon theology is conveyed in a way enjoyable for any age. (8 minutes, color, 16 mm—Rental $15.50)

Trick Films Productions, Prague, Czechoslovakia
Producer: Frantisek Vystreil

From: Brooklyn Public Library Film Department
178 Eastern Parkway
Brooklyn, New York 11238

THE DETACHED AMERICANS   This film examines the case of a New York murder. Thirty-eight onlookers watch a man stab a woman to death. The onlookers do nothing to help the woman because they do not want to get involved. (33 minutes, black and white, 16 mm—Rental $10.00)

Writer: John Knots; Narrator, Harry Reasoner

From: Mass Media Ministries
2116 North Charles Street
Baltimore, Maryland 21218

Or: 1714 Stockton Street
San Francisco, California 94133

HUNGER IN AMERICA   About 30 million out of 200 million Americans live in poverty which is incompatible with the basic freedom guaranteed to every American. This is a special CBS News report which examines four poverty areas in the United States, in one of the most startling presentations ever made. (54 minutes, black and white, 16 mm—Rental, inquire)

From: Carousel Films, Inc.
        1501 Broadway
        New York, New York 10036

THE SEEKERS   Study of drug addiction, marijuana and LSD. This is a successful eye opener for parents, and an emotional and scientific case against drug use. (31 minutes, color, 16 mm)

From: New York State Narcotic Control Commission
        Stuyvesant Plaza
        Albany, New York 12203

NIGHT AND FOG   This film possesses greater visual and moral impact in its subject area than any film in the industry. It presents a picture of German prison camp life during World War II, through which it raises the question of personal responsibility. Color footage of present-day Germany and black and white photography from the actual wartime situation create a dialogue between past and present, while pervasive camera motion from left to right communicates a sense of the relentless nature of suffering. *Night and Fog* demonstrates what man at his worst can do to man. It implies that an uncritical value system is criminal. (31 minutes, color or black and white Como films and Argos films)

From: Contemporary Films, Inc.
        267 West 25th Street
        New York, New York 10001

Or: 614 Davis Street
         Evanston, Illinois 60201

Or: 1211 Polk Street
         San Francisco, California 94109

TELEKETICS   A series of exciting 16 mm films of 9 to 12 minutes for discussion have been produced by St. Francis Productions. Some of these unusual films explore the meaning of the sacraments in a fresh, vital manner, while others deal with the critical dilemmas of war and peace, love and hate, loneliness and anxiety. These are some of the most dynamic audio-visual encounters for serious study.

From: St. Francis Productions
         1229 So. Santee Street
         Los Angeles, California 90015

Or: Association Films
         512 Burlington Avenue
         LaGrange, Illinois 60525

CHORAL READING FOR A PATRIOTIC SUNDAY
"And No One Asked"

READER   "In the beginning God created the heavens and the earth . . . And God saw that the light was good and God divided the light from the darkness . . . God called the light Day, and the darkness he called Night. And there was evening and there was morning, [the first day . . .] And God said, 'Let us make man in our image, after our likeness.' So God created man in his own image" (Genesis 1:1, 3–5, 26, 27).

VOICE   Was he white, yellow, or black? In the image of God
created He him.

VOICE   Was he Catholic, Protestant, or Jew?

READER   It doesn't say—only that He created man.

CHORUS (*full*)   Man was created man,
Different from fish or four-footed animal,
Different in color
But still man,
Wanting the same things.

VOICE   Food to eat.

VOICE   A place to sleep.

VOICE   Land to work, to live on, to build.

CHORUS (*full*)   A better world for his young,
And he got that better world
Because man worked with man.

VOICE   To build a home,

VOICE   To make the first wheel,

VOICE   To bring the first fire.

VOICE   And it was man working with man
Who built the town and the nation,

VOICE   The little house and the skyscraper,

VOICE   The wagon and the streamliner,

VOICE   The arching bridge and the 747.

CHORUS (*medium*)   And no one asked
Was he black or white,
Was he Catholic or Protestant or Jew,
No one—but the sick in mind.

VOICE   We built a nation, powerful and glorious,
Because man worked with man.

VOICE   The English at Plymouth,

VOICE   The Dutch in New Amsterdam,

VOICE   The Protestants in New England,

VOICE   The Catholics in Maryland.

CHORUS (*full*)   And we fought the Revolution
So man could live with man

In freedom, in peace.

CHORUS (*low*)   And no one asked
At Valley Forge and Saratoga
Was he black or white,
Was he Catholic or Protestant or Jew
No one, but the sick in mind.

VOICE   When the slaves in the South in their pain and suffering
Cried for freedom, they sang,

CHORUS (*high*)   When Israel was in Egypt land
Let my people go.
Oppressed so hard they could not stand,
Let my people go.
Go down, Moses, way down in Egypt land,
Tell ole Pharaoh to let my people go.

VOICE   The Protestant Negro and the white Jew
Yearn for freedom
Because Freedom belongs to all men,
Not to one color, not to one religion.

VOICE   In the pain and suffering
Did the wounded Protestant of Iowa
Fighting in the Korean hills, ask
"Whose blood are you pouring into my veins?
So that I may live?"

VOICE   Did the black gunner cutting his way
Through the jungles of Viet Nam, ask,
"Who made the gun, who filled this bullet?"

CHORUS (*medium*)   No one asked on the fighting front,
Is he black or white,
Is he Catholic or Protestant or Jew,
No one—but the sick in mind.

VOICE   I went to a movie last week,

RESPONSE   She saw Sidney Poitier, Negro.

VOICE   And I wore my new cotton dress.

RESPONSE   The cotton was picked by a black man in the South.

VOICE   I rode down by bus.

RESPONSE   Every race, every color, every religion was on that bus with her.

VOICE   And met my friend. We were hungry and went in for lunch.

RESPONSE   The man who served them was a Swede and Protestant.

VOICE   After the movies, I came home, turned on the TV, and watched my favorite programs.

RESPONSE   And saw Buddy Hackett, a Jew; Marlo Thomas, Catholic; Johnny Carson, a Protestant; and Bill Cosby, a black man.

VOICE   And I thought to myself what a wonderful world this was with so many different people helping me to be healthy and happy and how much I owed them.

CHORUS (*full*)   And she didn't ask once that day, on the bus, in the movies, in her home,
Is he black or white,
Is he Catholic or Protestant or Jew,
No one would—no one, but the sick in mind.

CHORUS (*high*)   The sick in mind, the sick in mind, the sick in mind, who are the sick in mind?

VOICE   In the old days they threw the Christians to the lions,

VOICE   They slaughtered the Jews in their homes,

VOICE   They drove the blacks into slavery.

CHORUS (*low*)   They were the sick in mind.

CHORUS (*full*)   They are the same today.

VOICE   They killed the Polish Catholics in prison camps.

VOICE   They killed the German Jews on their streets.

VOICE   They made slaves of Czech Protestants in their factories.

CHORUS (*high*)   They divided man from man with hate.

CHORUS (*low*)   They are the sick in mind.

CHORUS (*medium*)   They live in our midst today.

VOICE   They gang-up on a Jewish boy.

VOICE   They put a swastika on a Catholic Church.

VOICE   They smash up a Protestant pulpit.

VOICE   They won't give a black a job.

CHORUS (*full*) They are the sick in mind.
VOICE Would you get close to a person with smallpox?
VOICE Would you touch a boy who had scarlet fever?
CHORUS (*full*) Will you listen to the one who is sick in mind?
  Will you listen to the one
  Who divides black from white,
  Protestant from Catholic from Jew?
VOICE What are you missing?
CHORUS (*full*) Man divided from man,
  Man fighting against man,
  Has taken it from you
VOICE What have you?
  Man living with man,
  Man working with man,
  Gave it to you.
CHORUS (*high*) In all your deeds, in all your thoughts,
  In all you say, in all you do,
  Remember this—
READER "And God created man in his own image, in the image of
  God created he him" (1:27).
CHORUS (*full*) And it doesn't say he was white
  It doesn't say he was black,
  It doesn't say he was a Catholic or a Protestant or Jew.
  It just says, He created man—
  That's all of us.[36]

INTERRUPTING TESTIMONIALS
Can the World Be Made Better?

MINISTER'S INTRODUCTION Let us face honestly the question, "Is
there any hope for a better world? Is there any hope for a war-

less world, without the threat of invasion or nuclear destruction? Is it an empty dream to hope for a society without crime
or human folly, cruelty or graft, hostility or violence?"

INTERRUPTER I (*from a place in the congregation*) Preacher, I'll
answer that. Of course, there's no hope! Read the newspapers!
Listen to the TV newscasts! How can anyone with intelligence
think that the world can be another Garden of Eden? There
have always been wars and rumors of wars and there always
will be—the Bible says so! There has always been crime and
there always will be. The only difference now is that all of
this is on a larger scale. I see no hope. I'm very pessimistic,
and we all have a right to be.

MINISTER Friend, you articulate the feelings of untold numbers
of people. If I hear you right, are you saying that as long as
human beings are capable of iniquity, the world will not be
any better; that there is no use trying? we waste our energy
and money trying to improve conditions?

INTERRUPTER I You read me right! We might as well try to make
a brick into a diamond, or a subzero day into 100 degree
weather as to try to make this world better. The best any of
us can do, it seems to me, is take it the best we can, with as
much grace and fortitude as possible, and look out for Number One.

INTERRUPTER II (*from another place in the congregation*) Well,
let me say, "I don't agree." I'm not quite as pessimistic as our
friend who has been speaking. Granted there seems to be little hope of making a better world, yet perhaps we can keep
things from getting worse. If crime increases, we can take
steps to decrease it. If the dike breaks, we can build a new one.
The world may not be going forward as we would like, yet
if we work devotedly and support efforts that are good and
productive in character, we can at least keep it from going
backwards.

INTERRUPTER III Reverend, may I speak my view? Certainly, I can
appreciate the views of our two interrupters. Nevertheless, I

believe we should take the long-range view of things. We cannot look just to the last immediate years. If we will look back 100 years, 300 years or even 10,000 years, we can see that the world is better now than it was; therefore it can be better in the future than it is now. There was a time when 90 percent of the human beings were ill-fed, overworked, treated like animals and died young. A far greater proportion of the population is removed from stark need now than ever before. To be sure there are valleys and peaks. History reveals that mankind regresses periodically, but never to the degree it once knew; than mankind moves forward to higher elevations. I am optimistic, because it is in man's nature to improve his world.

MINISTER   Thank you for that hopeful contribution.

Perhaps it would be good if we looked for an answer from the source of our Christian faith and hope. A close reading of the New Testament seems to indicate that the early Christians had no hope for improving the world they lived in. At least, for example, they never talked about getting rid of slavery; they just treated a slave as though he was a brother. They never tried to organize a movement to assassinate the Emperor; they just refused to worship him. They never tried to get rid of the vice that made Corinth notorious; they apparently organized no agency to fight it; they just refused to participate in it. Ultimately the world they lived in was all turned upside down.

INTERRUPTER IV   But Reverend—that is all very strange to us in the twentieth century. It is naive to think entrenched evils can be overturned, unless there are organized efforts and well-planned demonstrations and campaigns of pressure. Such indifference to the apparent state of the world, as you have related, is shocking and un-Christian to me. How could a Christian possibly live without hope for a better world?

MINISTER   Let me clarify a point—which is the nitty-gritty of it all. The early Christians had hope, but they didn't hope for a better world. They hoped for a *new* world, not *another* world beyond this one, beyond death, not a *different* world with none of the familiar landmarks—earth, sea, stars, people. They hoped for a *new* world—the same world, completely transformed—not by man but by God's love and spirit.

INTERRUPTER IV   This is double talk, I don't understand what you mean!

MINISTER   Perhaps you will understand better if you think of an individual, someone in your experience who years ago had no light in his eye, no spring in his step, no lilt in his voice, no purpose in his days, just a depressed, blank sort of existence. To yourself you concluded, "There is a man with his future behind him." Then you saw him again recently—alive, alert, full of interest. You said to him, "You're a new man. What happened to you? What did you do?" You didn't mean, of course, that he was another man for he had the same body, same features, same history, same personality. Yet, he was different enough in attitudes and spirit as to be a new person! Perhaps his reply to your question, "What did you do?," was "I didn't do anything. But something happened to me—something was done to me. I fell in love." Or, "I walked into a job that I have wanted to do all my life, and I have put my talent to work." Or, "I saw what life is all about for the first time." Or, "I was picked out of the dumps by God. Now I am a new man."

Now, this is what the first Christians hoped would happen to the world. They didn't expect that it would be another world, but they hoped that God would make it a new world. They expected it to happen in their lifetime. It didn't. It hasn't. Whether it will sometime in the future, we do not know. But this much we do know: wherever there is a new man or woman in Christ, there is the possibility of a new world where he is.

TESTIMONIAL I   I've seen what you're talking about happen. The university where I used to teach was at rock-bottom. The morale was bad, students were undisciplined and rebellious, the

spirit of the faculty was low, there was division in the administration, enrollment dropped and huge indebtedness followed.
The trustees did everything possible to save the school. Finally,
a new president was brought to the leadership. No one thought
he could do anything to remedy the situation. However, he
was a "new man in Christ," and within two years there was a
"new" school. By his being the kind of person he was, the
life of the school was transformed.

TESTIMONIAL II   I have a testimony to add to that about a church
that was literally dead. The church had financial difficulties
because the members seemed to have no interest or dedication;
they neither attended nor served. Then a new minister came.
In a quiet way he began telling the people about the love of
God, and moving among the people with a humble, kind,
Christlike manner, until the church took on new life—in truth
was made "new." Oh, it's still the same old building, in the
same old place, but it is a "new" church in every aspect, because of a "new man in Christ."

TESTIMONIAL III   My family was near the breaking point several
years ago. It seemed that nothing would be able to hold it
together. We were all at odds with one another. Efforts were
made by us in the family, by our friends outside the family.
We even went to a counselor for help—all was in vain. We
split up. Our son came home from college one semester. While
there, something happened to him. He has a new boy, and
before long he had us all communicating with one another
again all together. We became a part of this larger family, the
church, and we are now a new family, thank God. Oh, we
have the same problems, the same human difficulties, the
same people to live with—but we have a new relationship because we are a new people.

MINISTER   Thank you for these testimonies of God's spirit. If
God can do this through one person, think of what he could
do through a group of people, scattered into the network of
society, each with his or her parish of influence. This is our
Christian vocation.

I am not suggesting you stop your efforts to improve the government, or the school system, or your community. However, I am suggesting that the new world begins when we each one become a "new creature" in Christ. When we are, we will do everything to make the world better. The real changes and the vital changes are not made by people who make the loudest noise, or even by those who think they are affecting the course of human affairs. Transformation comes as the unanticipated by-products of lives that are possessed by Christ's spirit of love, integrity and selflessness. From these perhaps we will see the vision of St. John, ". . . I saw a new heaven and a new earth; for the first heaven and the first earth were passed away . . ." (Revelation 21:1).

CHOIR SINGS   "The Impossible Dream"

DRAMATIC POETRY
A Divine Drama

All the world is a stage and all of us are players.
Happy are we when we know our roles and seek to play them well.
But to know our roles, we must of first importance
See a vision of the play.
Each holy day we are but striving to relive
The Holy Days and Weeks and Years of long ago.
The climactic act of history,
God's greatest drama—
So let the vision shine again—
The stage, the play, the Acts of God.
The Drama of Eternity.

Where should we start?
Act One. The house is dark,
The play begins.

When faith opens the curtain on history, the leading actor is already on stage. "In the beginning God . . . ." Without Him there would be no faith, there would be no stage, there would be no history. For it is not immutable god which is revealed. It is God: moving, breathing, walking, speaking. It is God: in the act of creation. "In the beginning God created the heavens and the earth . . ." (Genesis 1:1).

That which He has created is His. Faith says with the Psalmist, "The earth is the Lord's and the fulness thereof, the world and those who dwell therein" (Psalm 24:1).

Who will dispute God's ownership of that which He has made? Who is there to dispute it? No one was "in the beginning" with God. Who, then, is this on stage who writes and speaks of God as though apart from Him? As though a separate being? Now we see. His name is Man, a creation of God's hand, the very image of God's glory . . . molded from a lump of clay. What is man? An infinitesimal speck upon a fleck of dust, hurtling through endless space, yet with a mind, a heart, a will, a deathless soul.

Act One, Scene One is not yet through
Until the plot is clear—
God and Man in Conflict,
God and Man in conflict face to face.

Free agent is this Man
To spit at God if he so choose,
To blaspheme or ignore.
As we sit in breathless silence
Wondering what next,
We see a face;
And in the vision is revealed that Man is Me.

I am he!
Not spectator
But actor
It is God and I . . . in conflict now.
The curtain falls.

With greater interest than before
We read the program
Which foretells
Act Two. "Man's Way with God."
Act Three, "God's Way with Man."

The action now restored
The play moves on in rapid flight.
Man stones the Prophets,
Beats the slaves,
And calls it "Divine Will."
He steals and cheats and lies and kills,
And prays, "Oh Lord, be with me still."

"God helps those who help themselves,"
He mutters by his cozy fire.
"Don't get me wrong—
It's good to share—
Here's five for Church and five for CARE."

Man's way with God is all too clear—
A pious front and sweet veneer;
But underneath—
Rebellion, hate, and lust and greed
That only wait for social sanction,
The hair-fine trigger
That would bomb the "Reds" and lynch the "nigger."
Guilt, Rebellion, Sin and Evil
Man's way with God is clear

Ignore Him, turn your back and close your ears.
If still His pleading voice is heard

Then plot and plan and prove you can contrive
A way to kill the God who dares to
Judge your self-directed will.

Stop the vision, I protest
These things I have not, can not, will not do
Not me.

His answer is a silence—
Like my own which failed to lift a helping hand
While passing down the road that day where lay
My brother, beat and robbed.

"Oh God of mercy, now I know
It's I, this man that treats Thee so!
At last I feel the passion of this drama
Tell me what to do.
The certain end I cannot stand to see.
Guilt on Guilt. My guilt will surely drive me mad!
But lost and damned,
I must not, cannot be.
Move on! Move the Drama on! I pray."

Act Three, "God's Way with Man."
The Central Actor
Now has changed His form;
Where only spirit was before,
There now is flesh—
A living Word for Man to see.

He speaks:
"The meek be blessed
And those who mourn—
Forgive and be forgiven."
No man spake like this before.
"Our Father . . .
Hallowed be Thy Name."
Our Father! Who?

The God of Love?
God loves this guilty heart of mine?
His love will seek, forgive, restore?
He bares His feet and runs the road to meet
A dissipated Prodigal.
It cannot be! It is a lie! Not even God could love like that.
This pious man who speaks so fair of God, so wise of man
Will prove to be like all the rest of men.
He seeks to hypnotize, to trick and rule us,
But He, like all the rest, will pass away.
We will see the end of Him.

Let's watch Him now—
Before His peers accused,
Condemned.
Ha Ha! I told you so.
A Cross! Foul means of certain death.
He speaks:
One word alone,
"Forgive them for they do not know."
A spear!
A tomb!

A silent tomb. Surely now it's over, but the curtain doesn't fall, the vision lingers. The darkness on the stage surpassed now only by the starless midnight in my guilty heart.

"And when the sabbath was past, Mary Magdalene, and Mary the mother of James, and Salome, bought spices, so that they might go and anoint him. And very early on the first day of the week they went to the tomb when the sun had risen. And they were saying to one another, 'Who will roll away the stone for us from the door of the tomb?' And looking up, they saw that the stone was rolled back; for it was very large. And entering the tomb, they saw a young man sitting on the right side, dressed in a white robe; and they were amazed. And he said to them, 'Do

not be amazed; you seek Jesus of Nazareth, who was crucified.
He has risen, he is not here; see the place where they laid him'"
(Mark 16:1–6).

An empty tomb!
An empty tomb?
Oh God, Oh God,
Oh God above! It's true!
Shout it to the ages—
The victory belongs to God.
Not until You took my life did I begin to live.
You tore away my pride,
Stripped naked
Now at last I see
The face of God,
His Will,
His Way,
The Drama of Eternity.

No final curtain ends this play.
His Way is one without an end—
The Way of Faith,
Of Growth,
Of love for God and fellow men.
With each confession of man's faith
This drama is relived,
Man's way with God,
God's way with Man
New Life He gives.
He's calling you—
Take up your cross and follow Him—
Your self is all you have to give.[37]

Section 4

MUSIC SOURCES

Songs

Recordings

Resources

Song Index

CONTEMPORARY SONGS

Listed here are a few of the most generally acceptable and usable songs. An exhaustive listing is impossible because much is being written daily. Resources of records and hymnals for other songs are also included. The addresses of the publishers appear at the end of this section.

OPENING SONGS

"Praise God, Hurray" A snappy, catchy, interesting tune that has real life and rhythm. "Praise God, hurray, that in this day I see myself . . ." It is brief and can be readily learned by choir and congregation. Text by Don MacNeill; Music by Daniel Moe (0-4817A); Carl Fischer, Inc.

"Here We Are" Joyful, peppy fellowship song appropriate for opening of worship and might best be utilized with congregation singing the refrain and a director or choir singing the verses. In recording, *Mass For Young Americans;* F.E.L. Church Publications.

"Clap Your Hands" An excellent opening song of praise, based on Psalm 47. Achieves meaningful participation of worshipers by not only singing refrain, but body motion of clapping as well. The choir or a soloist may sing the verses. Lyrics and music written by Raymond Robert Repp. Included in *Hymnal For Young Christians,* and on record: *Mass For Young Americans,* both available from F.E.L. Church Publications.

"Shout From the Highest Mountains" "Shout from the highest mountains, the glory of the Lord." Appropriately it has a strong, rhythmic beat. A soloist or choir in a series of meaningful verses invites the congregation to sing the praise in refrain. Good opening song. Lyrics and music written by Raymond Robert Repp. Included in

Hymnal For Young Christians, and on record: *Mass For Young Americans,* both available from: F.E.L. Church Publications.

"Sing, People of God!"   Fresh, pulsating rhythmic praise song, appropriate for opening of worship service. Can be sung by congregation, or be used as an anthem by a specialty group. Lyrics and music are by Sebastian Temple. Included in record album, distributed by the World Library of Sacred Music, Inc.

"Glorious God"   The words attempt to describe the greatness of God, and our response in adoration in worship. A very good processional hymn. Lyrics and music are by Sebastian Temple. Included in a record album, distributed by the World Library of Sacred Music, Inc.

"Thank You, Jesus"   A song of thanksgiving for Jesus' life, teachings and love. It could be used either as a congregational hymn or choral anthem. Appropriate for opening praise, or communion text. Lyrics and music are by Sebastian Temple. Included in a record album, distributed by the World Library of Sacred Music, Inc.

"Today Is the Day"   Joyous mood of celebration in response to God's love. Christ came to bring us peace, therefore, "you gotta love your brother, gotta love one another, spread joy through the land." Suitable for opening praise song for worship. Written by Neil Blunt. In *Today,* Louisville Area Council of Churches. (Also on record from same source, sung by Agape Singers.)

OFFERTORY SONGS

"All That I Am"   Especially fine words for dedication or offertory hymn. It is brief, "all that I am . . . I give to you today." In recording, *Sing People of God* by Sebastian Temple. World Library of Sacred Music, Inc.

"Take My Hands"   This music is beautiful and most appropriate for dedication of life or offering. In recording, *Sing People of God* by Sebastian Temple. World Library of Sacred Music, Inc.

"Stranger, Share Our Fire"   Five verses of most fitting words by James Hearst, set to very appealing music by Daniel Moe. Congregational song or choral anthem. Augsburg Publishing Company.

"Of My Hands" "I give to Thee, O Lord." Quiet, brief, meaningful. A good offertory song. Can be sung by congregation or specialty group. Included in *Hymnal For Young Americans,* and on record: *Mass For Young Americans,* both available from F.E.L. Church Publications.

PRAYER SONGS AND RESPONSES

"Praise Response" The words of the traditional Gloria Patri set to contemporary music. Included in *Hymnal For Young Americans,* and on record: *Mass For Young Americans,* both available from F.E.L. Church Publications.

"Prayer For Mercy" The traditional *Kyrie,* set to contemporary music. Text is petition for Christ's mercy. In recording *Mass For Young Americans;* F.E.L. Church Publications.

"The Lord's Prayer" Several new tunes to the traditional prayer are very appealing. A modern chant is included in recording, *Mass For Young Americans;* F.E.L. Church Publications. Another very appealing arrangement is recorded by Agape Singers in *Today,* Louisville Area Council of Churches.
Still another beautiful interpretation with triumphant mood is in recording from *King of Kings,* called "The Prayer of Our Lord," an appropriate anthem. On soundtrack recording *King of Kings,* Metro-Goldwyn-Mayer.

"Angelic Song" New music and rhythm gives new life to the traditional *Sanctus,* "Holy, Holy, Holy, Lord God of Hosts." In recording, *Mass For Young Americans.* F.E.L. Church Publications.

"Hear, O Lord" Prayer petition in quiet, folk-type music. Not a difficult tune for unison congregational singing, or choral call to prayer. Three verses and refrain. Included in *Hymnal For Young Christians* and on record: *Mass For Young Americans,* both available from F.E.L. Church Publications.

"Free Me, Release Me, O Lord" Chant of absolution; appropriate following prayers of confession. Beautifully arranged by Daniel Moe. Words by Don and Nancy MacNeil. In *Worship For Today*—an ecumenical service. Carl Fischer, Inc.

"Listen" "The Words of Men Become the Words of God." Response following the reading of the scriptures. In *Worship For Today* by Daniel Moe and Don MacNeill. Carl Fischer, Inc.

"Prayer For Peace" Usable as choral anthem, or with soloist singing the verses and congregation the refrain. Beautiful music, meaningful words. In recording: *Sing People of God* by Sebastian Temple. World Library of Sacred Music, Inc.

"Spirit Of The Living God" "Fall afresh on me . . . melt, mold, fill, use me . . ." Quiet, beautiful prayer. Very singable by congregation. By Daniel Iverson and Herbert Tovey. In *Chapbook,* The Bethany Press.

COMMUNION SONGS

"The Blessed Sacrament" Outstanding number in text and music; appropriate as invitation to communion at the Lord's Table. The words are acceptable to Protestant or Roman Catholic for they convey sharing Jesus' love, passion and resurrection and the unity we have in Him. In recording: *Sing People of God* by Sebastian Temple. World Library of Sacred Music, Inc.

"Sons of God" Invitation to "sons of God" to gather around the Table of the Lord. A praise hymn in pleasing rhythm. Appropriate communion hymn. Lends to specialty group singing verses and congregation the refrain. In recording *Mass For Young Americans;* F.E.L. Church Publications.

"Let Us Break Bread Together" Negro spiritual appropriate for communion. Deeply meaningful and moving. Can be used as congregational song, solo, or specialty group. In *Hymns For Now;* Board For Young People's Work of the Lutheran Church, Missouri Synod (Resources For Youth Ministry).

"Bread of Life" "When all the world is blind in wrong. . . . the Father sent His only Son . . . A banquet table He has laid. . . ." The words of this song are so utterly appropriate as a congregational song for communion. In book, *Today's Songs for Today's People,* published by The Liturgical Conference.

"Song of the Lamb of God" (*"Agnus Dei"*) New melody and rhythm to traditional Roman Catholic chant about "Lamb of God

Who takes away the sins of the world." Ecumenically acceptable. In recording: *Mass For Young Americans;* F.E.L. Church Publications.

"Said the Lord" Appropriate words and music. Perhaps most successfully rendered by a choir doing the verses and the congregation the chorus. In recording: *Mass For Young Americans;* F.E.L. Church Publications.

"In Christ There Is No East or West" Emphasizes the oneness in Christ which transcends the barriers between people for, "in Him shall true hearts everywhere, their high communion find." A great song, though not a recent composition, it fits the contemporary flavor. Edward Marks Music Corp.

"Take Our Bread" "Take our bread . . . our hearts . . . our lives . . . O Father." A fine communion hymn. By Joseph Wise, World Library of Sacred Music, Inc.

CLOSING SONGS

"Follow Christ" Usable as a dedication hymn—and possibly for the opening of worship. Has appealing harmony and significant words. In recording *Sing, People of God* by Sebastian Temple. World Library of Sacred Music, Inc.

"That's For Me" An appropriate dedication song, with words affirming a positive response to new life in Christ. The words testify to the difference Jesus makes. Included in recording and music score, *Tell It As It Is* by Ralph Carmichael and Kurt Kaiser, Word, Inc.

"Pass It On" "It takes a spark to get a fire burning . . . Each lighted coal, lights those around it." So with those who know God's love, hence the theme, "Pass on the Word of love." An outstanding number with melodious tune and close harmony. Good as a closing song. Singable by congregation or specialty group. Included in recording and music score, *Tell It As It Is* by Ralph Carmichael and Kurt Kaiser, Word, Inc.

"Love Is Surrender" We can sing and shout about love, but it doesn't mean a thing without surrender to God's will. True love is obedient. An appropriate closing hymn. Specialty group or congregation. Included in recording and music score, *Tell It As It Is* by Ralph Carmichael and Kurt Kaiser, Word, Inc.

GENERAL WORSHIP SONGS

"Blowin' In the Wind" Beautiful penetrating music which has become the hymn of peace around the world. It summarizes in nine brief questions the infinitude of human inhumanity. The answer blowin' in the wind goes unheard by apathetic man. By Bob Dylan (Peter, Paul and Mary), Whitmark and Sons, Pepamar Music Corporation, c/o Warner Bros.

"Kumbaya" "Someone's crying, praying, singing—so come by here, Lord." A quiet chant, loved by young people. In Joan Baez Songbook, Ryerson Music Publishers, Inc.

"There's a World Out There" "The Lord gave us ears and eyes to see our world cryin', dyin'. . . . The Lord calls us to listen, listen." A peppy song that carries this strong message in appealing harmonies. A specialty group can probably handle this best with congregation singing refrain. Published by Darrell Faires.

"Brothers Be" We are one in the Fatherland of God. This is the love of unity the song expounds, and urges us to seek such love in our hearts. This is an exceptionally beautiful folk-type song with quiet, penetrating mood and words. Written by Carol Lichtefeld, Mary Hunt, and Sam Bateman; included in Agape Singers volume and record, *Today*. Louisville Area Council of Churches.

"I Am the Way" Meaningful lyrics centered around the quotation of Jesus, "I Am the Way." Set to beautiful harmony that presents antiphonal possibilities between men and women, or choir and congregation. Written by M. Wynne; included in the Agape Singers volume *Today*, and a record by same title both available from Louisville Area Council of Churches.

"Check Him Out" and "What's God Like" These belong in sequence. The first song affirms that God means different things to different people. Hence, we should "check Him out" before dismissing Him. The second song is a choral reading method depicting outgrown views of God, for God is love, light and is eternal.

This appears to be best for a specialty group rendition including a narrator and soloist. Composed by Ralph Carmichael and Kurt Kaiser. Included in *Tell It As It Is*. Score or recording (LIGHT LS-5512 LP) available from Word, Incorporated.

"Master Designer"   Another appealing song with lyrics about nature's origin—stars in the night, tall mountains, and the wonders we behold. There must be a plan and a master designer. The music is singable by a congregation or specialty group or for solo. Composed by Ralph Carmichael and Kurt Kaiser. Included in *Tell It As It Is*, Word, Inc.

"I Believe God Is Real"   The Lord we see with the eyes of soul. There is no doubt, we believe God is real, is the testimony of the meaningful song. Composed by Ralph Carmichael and Kurt Kaiser. Included in *Tell It As It Is*, Word, Inc.

"A New Mind"   Delightful harmonies to enforce the theme that new thinking is the need, based upon the Scripture passage, "Do not be conformed to this world, but be transformed by the renewal of your mind." Composed by Ralph Carmichael and Kurt Kaiser. Included in *Tell It As It Is*, Word, Inc.

"That's the Way It Is"   So much of the Christian life is absurd—losing life to find it, beauty being on the inside, turning the other cheek, the death of Jesus, but "that's the way it is." This majestic music is singable by the congregation led by a specialty group. Composed by Ralph Carmichael and Kurt Kaiser. Included in *Tell It As It Is*, Word, Inc.

"What Color Is God's Skin"   The text responds to questions a young son asks his father. Words witness to Christian view of brotherhood, and America's commitment. Beautiful music amplifies the meaning. Appropriate patriotic or race relations song. Usable as solo, anthem, and possibly for congregational singing. Book *Up With People* and included in recording, *Up With People* published by Pace.

"A New Tomorrow"   The theme is "Every gal and guy is needed for a new tomorrow." The sparkling enthusiasm creates affirmative action. The words challenge response. Usable as a closing song. Book

Up With People and included in recording *Up With People*, published by Pace.

"Freedom Isn't Free" Patriotic song, fast-moving, meaningful words emphasizing the price of freedom for every generation, past and present. Book *Up With People* and included in recording *Up With People*.

"You'll Never Walk Alone" This popular song from *Carousel* affirms that in the midst of storms, in the dark days of trouble, one is never alone. So walk on with "hope in your heart." A beautiful, beautiful song with a religious message. Can be sung by soloist, choir, and even congregation. Williamson Music Inc.

"Climb Every Mountain" Four verses of majestic words and music by Rogers and Hammerstein; from *Sound of Music*. The well-known words challenge one to climb on and on until one finds his dream—a dream that will need all the love we can give for as long as we live. These words have spirited overtones which make this song usable in contemporary worship. Williamson Music Inc.

"No Man Is an Island" "No man stands alone . . . we need one another." A real message in very appealing musical style. Appropriate as congregational song, anthem, or solo. Joan Whitney and Alex Kramer, Bourne Company.

"How Great Thou Art" These simply majestic words enumerate in four verses the greatness of God, in the vastness of the universe, in the beauty of nature, in the life and death of Jesus. A meaningful solo; outstanding anthem; and congregations like to sing it. Stewart Hine, Manna Music Inc.

"Amen, Amen" A joyous, syncopated number that the congregation can really participate in. Simple beat. Words picture six scenes of Jesus' life. Chorus follows each. Marion Downs, Arranger, Camp and Retreat Songs.

"I Feel the Winds of God Today" Uses the metaphor familiar to a sailor at sea. "Great Pilot . . . Thou wilt not let me drift." A beautiful, deeply moving hymn that has become a favorite. Christian Worship, Bethany Press.

"And I Will Follow" Based upon the figurative language of Psalm 23. Quiet melodious affirmation of God as Shepherd, and commitment to follow Him. Congregational song. In recording, *Mass For Young Americans,* and *Hymnal For Young Christians.* Both available from F.E.L. Church Publications.

"Forevermore" Refrain invites all to join in praise to God for his goodness. Verses depicting the love of God given in Jesus can be sung by soloist or choir. This is a very joyful, singable song. In recording, *Mass For Young Americans,* and *Hymnal For Young Christians.* Both available from F.E.L. Church Publications.

"The Impossible Dream" This is a great song of challenge and courage—to seek the impossible should be our quest. This is a powerful solo or choral anthem from the musical *Man of La Mancha* and usable for congregational singing. John Darion and Mitch Leigh, Sam Fox Publishing Company, Inc.

"Up With People" This song affirms that people are more important than things, so love them as they are. With soloist singing the verses and the congregation the refrains, it is a very challenging song. Book *Up With People* and included in recording *Up With People* published by Pace.

"We Are One In Jesus" The title is the basic theme. A most appropriate song for brotherhood or Christian unity emphasis, and for communion observance. In recording, *Sing, People of God,* by Sebastian Temple, World Library of Sacred Music, Inc.

"The Sound of Silence" A ballad depicting a vision and thoughts in the darkness. Hits hard at the "neon God" people worship. Best as a solo or specialty group song. By Paul Simon, included in the recording: *Sounds of Silence* (CS-9269), Columbia Records, C.B.S. Inc.

"Born Free" "Born free as the wind . . . Live free. Stay free." A beautiful, meaningful song for patriotic occasions. Can be used as congregational song, choral anthem, or solo. By Don Black and John Barry, Screen Gems—Columbia Music, Inc.

"Allelu!" "Everybody sing allelu! For the Lord has risen!" A joyous, triumphant song appropriate as praise hymn, especially for

Easter service. By Raymond Robert Repp, included in *Hymnal For Young Christians* and on recording: "Allelu!," both available from F.E.L. Church Publications.

"He's Got the Whole World In His Hands" Negro spiritual offering God's power, "for he's got the wind and rain . . . you and me brother . . . in His hands." Music is appealing, and not difficult. By Edward Bostner, Charles H. Hansen Music Company—California, Music Press.

"What the World Needs Now" The world needs *love*, there's too little of it. What we need is love, sweet love. The words are appropriate and the music moving and sufficiently easy for a congregation to sing. By Burt Bacharach and Hal David, Blue Seas Music, Inc. and Jac Music Company, Inc.

"Turn, Turn, Turn" Based upon the Scriptures of Ecclesiastes: "There is a time . . . to be born, a time to die." The refrain pleas, "Turn, Turn, Turn." A very meaningful song for closing dedication, or choral anthem. By Pete Seeger, Ludlow Music and Plymouth Music, and included in the recordings: *Byrd's Greatest Hits* (CS-9516), *Turn, Turn, Turn* (CS-9254), Columbia Records.

"If I Had a Hammer" "I've got a hammer of justice . . . bell of freedom, song of love." Swinging type of tempo and beat easy to follow. By Seeger-Hayes (Peter, Paul and Mary), Ludlow Music, and included in the recording: *(Ten) Years Together* (BS-2552), Warner Brothers Records.

"Let There Be Peace On Earth" Let peace begin with me. ". . . let me walk with my brother in perfect harmony." These simple words suggest the depth of meaning of this song. By Stu Miller and Jill Jackson, Jan-Lee Music.

"They'll Know We Are Christians By Our Love" We are one in the Spirit . . . We will walk and work with each other . . . spread the news of God. A fine closing hymn of commitment. Text and Music by Rev. Peter Scholtes. Included in *Hymnal for Young Christians,* on recording "They'll Know We Are Christians." Available from F.E.L. Church Publications.

"Let's Get Together" "Come on, people, now smile on your brother, everybody get together," is the theme of this timely song.

Good rhythm; not too difficult. Recorded by a number of popular recording artists. In "New Wine" produced by Southern California Conference, Methodist Church.

"Let's Give Adam and Eve Another Chance" The title tells the story. This is fast moving, and is perhaps best done by a specialty group. Gary Puckett and the Union Gap; Columbia Records Stereo 4S-45097.

"Who Will Answer?" One of the biggest and most difficult contemporary songs. It hurls the challenge, "Who will answer?" to a long list of present problems. This is a dramatic number requiring a capable soloist, plus choir or specialty group. Recorded by a number of popular artists including Ed Ames on Victor.

"Lonesome Valley" A Negro spiritual of three verses. "Jesus walked this lonesome valley by Himself. . . . We must walk it by ourselves." A very quiet, meditative, singable song. Recorded by Glenn Yarborough on Tradition label, and other artists.

"These Things Shall Be" "A loftier race . . . shall rise . . . with freedom in their souls. . . ." A powerful anthem for choir. In "Christian Worship," Bethany Press.

"Light One Little Candle" By George M. Sels and J. Malloy Roach, inspirational anthem in *Youth Sings*, Shawnee Press, Inc.

COMPLETE LITURGICAL MUSICAL PROGRAMS

Good News Developed by the Southern Baptist Church. Very appealing, with an evangelistic emphasis. Broadman Records.

Tell It As It Is Kurt Kaiser and Ralph Carmichael have combined to create a dynamic program of testimony, scripture and music. Word Inc.

The Winds of God   A contemporary liturgy for celebrating Holy Communion with appropriate folk songs and tunes. Youth Folk Mass.

Worship For Today   An ecumenical service, presented at the American Guild of Organist National Convention in 1968. Words by Don and Nancy MacNeill; Music by Daniel Moe. Carl Fischer Inc. No. 0-4817 A

The Easter Story   A product of West Side Chicago teen-agers who wrote songs in response to their first reading of the Passion Story. Act IV Productions.

Celebration of Man's Hope   A most unusual, unorthodox, "far-out" contemporary program written by Ed Summerlin. Has much youth appeal. Ed Summerlin.

The Light In the Wilderness   Dave Brubech has written and produced the music and text for this modern oratorio based upon the temptations and teachings of Jesus. (See record Decca DL 710,155 Stereo LP.)

Rock 'N' Roll Mass   Follows the traditions of Martin Luther of combining secular music with texts for worship. Available from F.E.L. Church Publications.

Contemporary Liturgy   Lutheran Student Association of America.

BOOKS OF CONTEMPORARY RELIGIOUS SONGS

Today Is the Day to Sing God's Song   Agape Singers, Vol. I, Louisville Area Council of Churches. Songs include: "Today Is the Day," "Emmanuel," "I Am The Way," "St. Francis' Prayer," "There Are But Three Things," "Brothers Be," "Lord's Prayer," "Lord of the Dance," "Called to Freedom," "When I Sing," "I'm Ready to Follow," "I Am The Good Shepherd," "Sow The Seed," "Joy In My Heart."

Listen   Agape Singers, Vol. II, Louisville Area Council of Churches. Songs include: "Shalom," "Rejoice," "The Thread of Life," "God Made The World," "Prayer to the Holy Spirit," "Alle-Alle," "Listen," "The Spirit Is A'movin," "Grow—Become," "Beatitudes," "Eternally Alive," "Irelander's Wish."

New Hymns For a New Day   RISK, Vol. II, Number 3, Youth Department, World Council of Churches. Songs include: "Jonah," "Amen," "The Devil Wore a Crucifix," "A Cry In The Night," "The Tree Springs to Life," "Bitter Was the Night," "Song of God's Presence," "Nicodemus," "Crucify That Man," "Bread In The Wilderness," "Question Song," "Song of the Lord Among Us," "Lord's Prayer," "What's That I Hear," "As Long As Men On Earth Are Living," "Thank You," "Hymn For Those In Captivity," "Oh Freedom," "We Shall Overcome," "The Strife Is O'er," "Joy Shall Come," "Laudamus."

Hymns Hot and Carols Cool   By Richard Avery and Donald Marsh, Proclamation Productions. Songs include: "Hey! Hey!," "Anybody Listening?" (Advent Carol), "Here We Go A-Caroling" (Advent), "Little Baby Boy" (Christmas Carol), "Mary, Mary" (Christmas Carol), "Take Time" (Epiphany Carol), "Hosanna, Hallelujah" (Palm Sunday Carol), "The Rebel" (Lenten Carol), "Christ the Lord Is Risen" (Easter Carol), "Is There A Holy Spirit" (Pentecost Hymn), "Jesus, White Boy, Thank You, Thank You" (Carol of Gratitude), "When I'm Feeling Lonely" (Personal Carol), "Gloria Patri," "Doxology."

Joy Is Like the Rain   By The Medical Mission Sisters, Vanguard Music Corporation. Recording available—AVANT GARDE AVM101. Songs include: "Joy Is Like the Rain," "Zaccheus," "Come Down, Lord," "It's A Long Road to Freedom," "Howl, My Soul," "Ten Lepers," "God Gives His People Strength," "The Wedding Banquet," "Pilgrim Song," "How I Have Longed," "Speak To Me, Wind."

New Songs For the Church—Book I   By Reginold Barrett-Ayres & Erik Routley, Galaxy Music Corp.

> Psalms: "Psalm 15," "O Clap Your Hands" (Psalm 47), "Jerusalem" (Psalm 122), "Psalm 126," "Psalm 130."
> Songs For Children: "The Kings," "Palm Sunday," "Children Go!," "We Thank You Lord," "Stomp and Shout," "The World I Walk In."

Ballads: "Where Is He?," "Gethsemane," "A Star Is Born," "Body and Blood," "God Is the Boss," "The World He Loves," "My Brother's Keeper."

Hymns, A Carol and The Blessings: "Working Days," "All Who Love and Serve Your City," "Christ Our Great King," "Our Risen Lord," "Lord Bring the Day to Pass," "Wedding Hymn," "Bethlehem Carol," "Aaronic Blessings."

Sing Around the Year Edited by Donald Swann, Galaxy Music Corp. "Here We Go To Bethlehem," "Standing In the Rain," "Every Star Shall Sing a Carol," "Jesu Parvule," "The Storke Carol," "Jubilate Domino," "Christmas," "The Devil Wore a Crucifix," "Psalm 95," "The Clock Carol," "Sanctus," "Judas and Mary," "Praise the Lord," "The Fruit of the Tree," "Dust, Dust and Ashes," "I Lie Down With God," "Lord of the Dance," "Benedictus."

Faith, Folk and Festivity By Peter Smith, Galliard Limited, Galaxy Music Corporation.

Advent: "Song and Dance," "When He Comes Back," "Ballad of the Son of Man," "Where?," "Go, Prophet, Go."

Christmas: "Sing High with the Holly," "Shepherds on Nothing Hill," "Don't Wait For An Angel."

Lent: "A Song for Lent," "We Find Thee Lord," "Nobody Dances."

Palm Sunday: "Processional for Palm Sunday," "When They Shouted Hosanna."

Holy Week: "Friday Morning," "Come and Climb the Mountain," "Good Friday," "Down Huddersfield Road," "Indifference."

Easter: "The Sun and the Hill" (Peter and John), "The Tree Springs to Life," "Celebration Song," "Christ Through the Waters," "Creation's Song."

Ascension: "The Promise," "I Will Be With You Always."

Pentecost: "The Day of the Spirit," "Fire Is Lighting Torch and Lamp at Night," "Bird of Heaven," "Thou Mastering Me," "You Were There."

Trinity: "The Trinity of Mutual Love," "Father In Heaven."

Harvest: "Lord of the Harvest," "Pop Goes The Money," "Wonderful Is Your Handiwork," "A Cry of Spirits," "Working Days," "Loving All In All For Us."

Remembrance: "The Killer," "The Crow on the Candle," "Vine and Fig Tree," "There Is A World."

All Saints: "We Thank You For the Memories," "Woman In the Bus," "Harvey," "How Can I Keep From Singing."

Festivity: "Let the Cosmos Ring."

Faith, Folk and Clarity   By Peter Smith, Galliard Limited, Galaxy Music Corp.

Songs of Faith and Worship

Christian Worship: "Praise To God," "Amazing Grace," "How Little I Am In It All," "The Lord's Prayer," "Thank You," "Standing In The Need of Prayer," "Kumbaya," "Let Us Break Bread Together," "Shout For Joy."

The Life of Christ: "Go Tell It On The Mountain," "Mary's Child," "Joys Seven," "Judas and Mary," "Son of Man," "Were You There?," "Hammering," "The Angel Rolled The Stone Away," "Love Is Come Again," "My Dancing Day," "Lord of the Dance," "Amen."

The Christian Life: "This Little Light of Mine," "Give Me Jesus," "Where Is God?," "I'm Troubled In Mind," "Have We Changed?," "Come All You Worthy Christian Men," "Simple Gifts."

Songs of Freedom and Concern

Freedom and Prejudice: "The Family of Man," "Our Town," "Kids' Color Bar," "Different From Us," "Del Gedanken Sind Frei," "Go Down Moses," "Oh Freedom."

Peace and War: "Gonna Lay Down My Sword and Shield," "I Want To Have a Little Bomb Like You," "Been On The Road So Long," "Across the Hills," "Grand and Gracious Feeling."

World Need: "When I Needed A Neighbor," "All My Trials," "Fair Shares For All," "Feed Us Now," "Half the World," "I've Got a Million Sisters," "One Man's Hands."

Social Concern: "There But For Fortune," "Devils and Lazarus," "The Threshold," "Mixed-Up Old Man," "My Neighbor," "Needle of Death," "Come Down Lord From Your Heaven," "Shelter," "There's No Room For Heaven Here," "We Shall Overcome."

Hymns and Songs   A supplement to *The Methodist Hymn Book*, Methodist Book Room (England). Sizeable collection of hymns used in England most of which were written in the present decade, also of songs not identifiable as hymns. An index of composers and copyright owners is included. Most of the selections are not among those better known in America; yet this is a usable and good resource.

Shout For Joy The Hymnal of the Chicago Theological Seminary. Songs include: "Build a Better World," "O Lord of All," "Celebrating the Beat," "Thank You God For Everything," "O God Whose Grandeur," "Rejoice In Celebration," "Every Now and Then," "Twenty-third Psalm," "The First Christmas," "The Peace of God," "Joy, Shout For Joy," "Morning Psalm," "Life and Breath."

Gonna Sing My Lord Joseph Wise, World Library of Sacred Music, Inc. Songs include: "Gonna Sing My Lord," "Sing Praises To The Lord," "Maleita's Song," "Lord, Have Mercy," "Take Our Bread," "Jesus, You Are Here," "We Are Your Bread," "We Will Hear Your Word," "God of My Life."

They'll Know We Are Christians By Our Love Rev. Peter Scholtes, F.E.L. Church Publications. Songs include: "Choose Life," "Take My Hand," "They'll Know We Are Christians," "There Once Was a Man," "We Gather Together," "Glory Be To Israel," "Holy, Holy, Holy," "Our Father," "Lamb of God."

Hand In Hand (13 liturgical folk songs) Joseph Wise, World Library of Sacred Music, Inc. Songs include: "Lift Your Voice," "Bread You Have Given Us," "Blessed Are Those," "You Fill The Day," "To Be Your Body," "The Lord Said To Me," "Yours Is Princely Power," "Let The Heavens Be Glad," "In Holy Splendor," "My People," "Peace, Joy, Happiness," "Yes To You, My Lord," "A New Commandment."

Hymns For Now Workers Quarterly, Volume 39, Number 1, Resources For Youth Ministry. Among the songs are: "Shalom," "Amen," "Thank You," "Lord of the Dance," "Sons of God," "We Shall Overcome," "Nicene Creed," "Oh Freedom," "A Cry In The Night," "Allelu."

Hymnal For Young Christians F.E.L. Church Publications. This contains the largest number of songs grouped as follows: Entrance

Songs, Offertory Songs, Communion Songs, General Liturgical Songs, Songs on the Psalms, Other Songs From Scripture, Songs for Children and Catechetical Songs.

Contemporary Music for Congregations published by Robert R. Sanks.

Folk Music: "The Innocents," "The Spirit of the Lord Is Upon Us," "Joy Is Now," "What Has Drawn Us Together," "The Rebel," "Take Time," "I Was Hungry," "It's a Long Hard Journey," "Allelulia," etc.

Jazz Music: "A Hymn After Quoist," "Come Praise Him," "We're Here To Sing Our Love For God," "God Give Us Your Peace," "Hello: And Did You Hear the Word?," "Bread," "God's Own Son," etc.

New Forms: "Design For Music With Body Movement," "Mass For Voices and Electronics," "Tape Circuit Diagram," "Lerna Landscapes."

New Wine Southern California Methodist Church Conference, c/o Bishop Gerald H. Kennedy, Los Angeles Area United Methodist Church. Songs include: "Sons of God," "Let's Get Together," "Magic Penny," "Lord of the Dance," "Turn, Turn, Turn," "I Can See A New Day," "Gift of Song," "Born Free," "The Spirit of the Lord," "This Land Is Your Land," "Hammer Song," etc.

More Songs From The Square Galliard Ltd. Twelve contemporary songs used in England, not broadly known in the United States of America.

Songs of Faith Joint Board of Christian Education of Australia and New Zealand. Ninety-two contemporary songs used in Australia and New Zealand.

Today Songs for Today's People edited by Ed Summerlin, The Liturgical Conference. Songs include: "Hey! Hey! Anybody Listening?," "Is There Hope?," "Bread of Life," "Joy Is Now," "Liberate Me," "The Spirit of the Lord Is Upon Us.'

Word Alive Edited by Edmund Banyard, Belton Books. Anthology of readings drawn from likely and unlikely sources for use in Christian education and worship. It includes songs, poetry and prose and is most usable.

Youth Sings   published by Shawnee Press, Inc.

RECORDINGS OF
CONTEMPORARY RELIGIOUS MUSIC

JAZZ RECORDS WITH RELIGIOUS THEMES:

Liturgical Jazz	ECCLESIA	ER101
My People (Duke Ellington)	CONTACT	CM1
Black, Brown and Beige (Duke Ellington)	CONTACT	CMI
Duke Ellington's Concert of Sacred Music	RCA VICTOR	LPM3582
Jazz Suite On the Mass Texts (Paul Horn)	RCA VICTOR	LPM3414
Jazz Man by Joe Masters	COLUMBIA	CL2598

FOLK RECORDS WITH RELIGIOUS THEMES:

Today (Agape Singers)	CP–1267A	
Listen (Agape Singers)	CP–1267B	
Rejoice! (General Theological Seminary Students)	SCEPTER Records	527
Joy Is Like the Rain (Medical Mission Sisters)	AVANT GARDE	AVM101
Praise the Lord In Many Voices, Vol. I "Mass of a Pilgrim People" (Sister Miriam Therese Winter and the Medical Mission Sisters)	AVANT GARDE	AVM102

Praise the Lord in Many Voices, Vol. II "Praise the Lord" (Mary Lou Williams) "Folk Songs For the Young In Spirit" (Paul Quinlon S. V.)	AVANT GARDE AVM103
Praise the Lord in Many Voices, Vol. III "Community Man" (Bruno Markaitis) "By Request" (Robert Edwin)	AVANT GARDE AVM104
Knock! Knock! (Medical Mission Sisters)	AVANT GARDE AVM109
I Know The Secret (Medical Mission Sisters)	AVANT GARDE AVM105
Keep the Rumor Going (Robert Edwin)	AVANT GARDE AVM106
Cool Living (John Yluisaker)	AVANT GARDE AVM107
American Mass Program (Father Rivers)	World Library Publications
A Man Dedicated To the Brotherhood of Man (Rivers)	World Library Publications
Sing! People of God, Sing!	World Library Publications
A Time to Keep (Billson)	World Library Publications
Gonna Sing, My Lord (Wise)	World Library Publications
Run Like a Deer (Paul Quinlon. Psalms in folk-rock style)	Friends of the English Liturgy
Funeral Folk Mass (Jan Mitchell)	Friends of the English Liturgy
20th Century Folk Mass	Fiesta FLD25000
Donald Swann Sings Songs of Faith and Doubt ("Lord of the Dance," "The Devil Wore a Crucifix," "The Rat Race," "Every Star Shall Sing a Carol," "The Mask I Wore," "Friday Morning"—Songs by Sydney Carter)	ARGO EAF48
Holy Ghost Reception Committee No. 9	PAULIST PRESS FRIENDSHIP PRESS

Sing Round the Year (Donald Swann)	GALAXY MUSIC CORPORATION
The Present Tense (Sydney Carter's Songs Sung by "Reflection," folk-rock group)	GALAXY MUSIC CORPORATION
Make a Joyful Noise (Complete Worship Service)	WOODMONT CHRISTIAN CHURCH Hillsboro Rd & Woodmert Bend Nashville, Tennessee 37215
Good News (Earl Grant)	DECCA 74811
(Staple Singers)	EPIC 26332
Up With People	PACE 1101 TAPE UB2024 PACE
Tell It As It Is (Kurt Kaiser Singers)	LIGHT LS5512 LP
Let's Give Adam and Eve Another Chance (Gary Puckett and the Union Gap)	COLUMBIA Stereo 4S45097
The Light in the Wilderness ("An Oratorio For Today," Dave Brubeck, pianist; William Justus, baritone; Miami University A Cappella Singers; Cincinnati Symphony Orchestra)	DECCA DL710, 155 Stereo LP DXSA7202
Mass In F Minor (The Electric Prunes)	REPRISE RS6275
Sing! People of God, Sing (Sebastian Temple)	ST. FRANCIS PRODUCTIONS Stereo SFPS–67–1
Mass For Young Americans (Ray Repp)	SR4M–6403 F.E.L. Church Publications

CONTEMPORARY EXPERIMENTS AND MUSIC INFORMATION RESOURCES

Probe
  Christian Associates of Southwest Pennsylvania
  220 Grant Street
  Pittsburgh, Pennsylvania   15219
The Center For Contemporary Celebration
  116 South Michigan Avenue
  Room 1600
  Chicago, Illinois   60603
F.E.L. Church Publications
  22 East Huron Street
  Chicago, Illinois   60611
Liturgical Conference
  1330 Massachusetts Avenue, N.W.
  Washington, D. C.
Galaxy Music Corporation
  c/o Rev. Paul Abels
  2121 Broadway
  New York, New York   10023
The Place
  c/o William R. Richards
  475 Riverside Drive
  Suite 420
  New York, New York   10027
Trafco
  c/o Rev. Sam Barefield
  1525 McGavock Street
  Nashville, Tennessee   37203

Glibe Urban Center
330 Ellis
San Francisco, California
Dr. W. H. McGaw, Jr.
Director of Communications
Western Behavioral Science Institute
1150 Silverado
La Jolla, California   92037
General Board of Evangelism
c/o Rev. Bill Garrett
Director of Youth Projects
General Board of Evangelism
1908 Grand Ave.
Nashville, Tennessee   37203
The Contemporary Mix
c/o Ed Summerlin
Box 242
Pleasant Valley
New York, New York   12569
Pace Magazine Feature—(SING OUT)
833 South Flower Street
Los Angeles, California   90017

INDEX OF SONGS

Song	Source	Page
"A New Mind"	Record, *Tell It As It Is*	215
"A New Tomorrow"	Record, *Up With People*	215
"And I Will Follow"	Record, *Mass For Young Americans*	217
"Battle Hymn of the Republic"	In most hymnbooks	24
"Blowin' In the Wind"	By Bob Dylan—Sheet Music—Whitmark and Sons	32, 214
"Born Free"	By Don Black and John Berry—Columbia Music	22, 217
"Bread of Life"	Book, *Today's Songs for Today's People*	63, 212
"Brothers Be"	Record, *Today*	214
"Celebration Song"	Book, *Faith, Folk and Festivity*	222
"Check Him Out"	Record, *Tell It As It Is*	214
"Clap Your Hands"	Record, *Mass For Young Americans*	209
"Climb Every Mountain"	Musical, *Sound of Music*	216
"Countin' My Blessings"	Fred Waring, Decca 74345, album, *God's Trombones*	39
"Follow Christ"	Record, *Sing, People of God*	213
"Freedom Isn't Free"	Record, *Up With People*	216
"Free Me, Release Me, O Lord"	Book, *Worship For Today*	211
"Give Me Your Tired, Your Poor"	Sheet Music, also Fred Waring recording	24
"Glorious God"	Record, *Sing, People of God*	210
"Go Tell It On the Mountain"	Book, *Songs of Faith*	17, 18, 223
"Hear, O Lord"	Book, *Hymnal For Young Christmas*	211
"Hear Our Prayer, O Lord"	Book, *Christian Worship*	20
"Here We Are"	Record, *Mass For Young Americans*	209
"He's Got the Whole World In His Hands"	By Edward Bostner—Charles Hansen Music Co.	29, 218
"How Great Thou Art"	By Stewart Hine—Manna Music Inc.	216
"I Am the Way"	Record, *Today*	214
"I Believe God Is Real"	Record, *Tell It As It Is*	215

PUBLISHERS' ADDRESSES

Act IV Productions
3535 W. Roosevelt Rd.
Chicago, Ill. 60601

Agape Singers
210 YMCA Building
Louisville, Ky. 40202

Augsburg Publishing Co.
57 E. Main St.
Columbus, Ohio 43215

Avant-Garde Records, Inc.
250 W. 57th St.
New York, N.Y. 10019

Belton Books
Lornehurst, 191 Creighton Ave.
East Finchley, London N. 2,
England

The Bethany Press
115 N. Jefferson Ave.
St. Louis, Mo. 63166

Board for Young People's Work
   of the Lutheran Church
Missouri Synod (Resources for
   Youth Ministry)
St. Louis, Mo. 63178

Bourne Company
136 W. 52nd St.
New York, N.Y. 10019

Broadman Records
127 9th Avenue N.
Nashville, Tenn. 37203

Camp and Retreat Songs
4075 S. Dearborn St.
Chicago, Ill. 60609

Columbia Records
CBS Inc.
51 West 52nd St.
New York, N.Y. 10019

Darrell Faires
1848 Bahama Ct.
St. Louis, Mo. 63136

F.E.L. Church Publications
22 E. Huron St.
Chicago, Ill. 60611

Fiesta Records Co., Inc.
1619 Broadway
New York, N.Y. 10019

Carl Fischer, Inc.
62 Cooper Square
New York, N.Y. 10003

Sam Fox Publishing Co., Inc.
1841 Broadway
New York, N.Y. 10023

Friendship Press
475 Riverside Dr.
New York, N.Y.   10023

Galaxy Music Corp.
2121 Broadway
New York, N.Y.   10023

Galliard, Ltd.
Southtown, Great Yarmouth
England

The Hymnal of the Chicago
  Theological Seminary
5757 S. University Ave.
Chicago, Ill.   60637

Jac Music Co., Inc.
15 E. 48th St.
New York, N.Y.   10017

Jan-Lee Music
Beverly Hills, Calif.

Joint Board of Christian Education of Australia and New
  Zealand
147 Collins St.
Melbourne, Victoria, Australia

The Liturgical Conference
1330 Massachusetts Avenue N.W.
Washington, D.C.

Ludlow Music Co.
10 Columbus Circle
New York, N.Y.   10019

Lutheran Student Association of
  America
327 S. La Salle St.
Chicago, Ill.   60610

Manna Music, Inc.
Box 1830
Hollywood, Calif.   90028

Edward Marks Music Corp.
136 W. 52nd St.
New York, N.Y.   10019

Methodist Book Room
2 Chester House
Pages Lane, Uswell Hill
London N 10, England

Music Press
1842 West Ave.
Miami Beach, Fla.   33139

Pace Music Co.
"Up With People"
833 S. Flower St.
Los Angeles, Calif.   90017

Paulist Press
400 Sette Drive
Paramus, N.J.   07652

Plymouth Music
17 W. 60th St.
New York, N.Y.   10023

Proclamation Productions
7 Kingston Ave.
Port Jervis, N.Y.   12771

Resources for Youth Ministry
P.O. Box 14325
St. Louis, Mo.   63178

Ryerson Music Publishers, Inc.
154 W. 14th St.
New York, N.Y.   10011

W. H. Sadlier, Inc.
11 Park Pl.
New York, N.Y.   10007

Robert R. Sanks
1121 University Ave.
Madison, Wis.   53715

Scepter Records (Blue Seas
   Music Co.)
254 W. 54 St.
New York, N.Y.   10011

Screen Gems-Columbia Music,
   Inc.
711 Fifth Ave.
New York, N.Y.   10022

Shawnee Press, Inc.
Delaware Water Gap,
   Penna.   18327

Southern California Methodist
   Church Conference
c/o Bishop Gerald H. Kennedy
Los Angeles Area United Methodist Church
5250 Santa Monica Blvd.
Los Angeles, Calif.   90029

Ed Summerlin
Box 242
Pleasant Valley, N.Y.   12569

Today, published by Louisville
   Area Council of Churches
YMCA Building
Louisville, Ky.   40202

Vanguard Music Corp.
250 W. 57th St.
New York, N.Y.   10019

Victor Records
RCA Corp.
155 E. 24th St.
New York, N.Y. 10010

Warner Brothers Records
400 Warner Blvd.
Burbank, Calif.   91505

488 Madison Ave.
New York, N.Y.   10022

Williamson Music, Inc.
609 Fifth Ave.
New York, N.Y.   10017

Word, Inc.
Box 1790
Waco, Texas   76703

World Council of Churches,
   Youth Dept.
150 Route de Ferney
1211 Geneva 20, Switzerland

World Library of Sacred Music,
   Inc.
2145 Central Parkway
Cincinnati, Ohio   45214

Youth Folks Mass
1620 Huron Ave.
San Mateo, Calif.   94401

SOURCE NOTES

SECTION 1—SERVICES FOR TODAY'S CHRISTIANS

[1] Adapted from Psalm 146. Used in First Christian Church, Reseda, California.

[2] Youth Service created by the youth of Central Christian Church, Memphis, Tennessee. Permission to print the words to "Blowin' In the Wind" by Bob Dylan was denied. The words may be found in sheet music published by Whitmark and Sons.

[3] "Voices of a World in Revolution" (a choral poem), by Phillip N. Linsell.

[4] By William A. Holmes *Tomorrow's Church.*

[5] Adapted from "Don Chen Magic Mass," St. Clemens Church, West 46th St., New York.

[6] Adapted from *Hymn of the Universe* by Pierre Teilhard de Chardin.

[7] Liturgy of the Washington Square Methodist Church, New York.

[8] "A Wedding Ceremony" by John Thompson, Pastor, First Congregational Church, Sarasota, Florida.

[9] Adapted from *The Common Ventures of Life* by Elton Trueblood.

SECTION 2—DEVOTION GUIDES

[10] By Jacquie Clingan.

[11] By Toki Miyashima.

[12] By Carl F. Burke *Treat Me Cool, Lord.*

[13] Ibid.

[14] By Kahlil Gibran *Jesus, the Son of Man.*

[15] Poem circulated at the poor people's rally in Old Town, Albuquerque, New Mexico.

[16] By Carl F. Burke *God Is For Real, Man.*

[17] Ibid.

[18] By Dr. Chester Pennington in *The Christian Athlete.*

[19] By Mary Lou Lacy *And God Wants People.*

[20] By Ernest Gordon *Through the Valley of the Kwai.*

[21] By Loren Eiseley *The Immense Journey.*

[22] By Alan Paton "Meditation for a Young Boy Confirmed."

[23] By John Courtney Murray "Freedom, Authority and Community."

[24] By the late William H. Alexander.

[25] By G. Edwin Osborn *The Glory of Christian Worship.*

[26] By Warren Lane Molton.

[27] By Wilferd A. Peterson *The Art of Living.*

[28] By Eric Butterworth *Discover the Power Within You.*

[29] By George Earl Owen in "Unified Promotion Bulletin."

[30] By Robert Raines *Creative Brooding.*

[31] By Georgia Harkness *The Glory of God.*

SECTION 3—SERMONS: SUCCESSFUL EXPERIMENTS

[32] From the Graduate Seminary Chapel of Phillips University, Enid, Oklahoma, by J. Daniel Joyce, Dean.

[33] Adapted from "The Christmas Cast" in *Catalyst.*

[34] By John Robert McFarland in *Pulpit Digest.*

[35] Based on material prepared by Rev. Donald Chichester and the youth of the First Presbyterian Church, Southampton, New York. Used by permission.

[36] By Morris Reich *American Unity* Jr. High School 186, Queens, 144-80 Barclay Ave., Flushing, N.Y. 11355.

[37] By Robert A. Fudge, late minister of Village Christian Church, Oklahoma City, Oklahoma.

BIBLIOGRAPHY—Books Related to Contemporary Worship (Other Than Song Books)

Bloy, Myron B., Jr. (Editor), *Multi-Media Worship* (Seabury Press, New York, 1969)

Boyd, Malcolm, *Are You Running With Me, Jesus?* (Holt, Rinehart and Winston, New York, 1965)

Brenner, Scott Francis, *Ways of Worship For New Forms of Mission* (Friendship Press, New York, 1968)

Brown, D. Mackenzie, *Ultimate Concern—Tillich in Dialogue* (Harper & Row, New York, 1963)

Burke, Carl, *God Is For Real, Man* (Association Press, New York, 1969)

————, *Treat Me Cool, Lord* (Association Press, New York, 1968)

Butterworth, Eric, *Discover the Power Within You* (Harper and Row, New York)

Cox, Claude, Article: "Christian Ethics in Current Rock Music" (*The Christian*, P.O. Box 179, St. Louis, Missouri 63166, August 10, 1969)

Gibran, Kahlil, *Jesus, the Son of Man* (Alfred A. Knopf, New York, 1956)

Harkness, Georgia, *The Glory of God* (Abingdon Press, Nashville, Tenn., 1943)

Hearn, Raymond, *Modern Psalms For Boys* (University of London Press, London, England, 1966)

Hegen, Robert, S.J. and Meyer, Anthony, S.J., *Discovery in Drama* (Paulist Press, Paramus, New Jersey and Association Press, New York, 1969)

Discovery in Film, Ibid.

Discovery in Song, Ibid.

Discovery in Word, Ibid.

Hersey, N. L., *Worship Services For Special Occasions* (Word Publishing Co., Waco, Texas, 1970)

239

Holmes, William A., *Tomorrow's Church* (Abingdon Press, Nashville, Tennessee, 1968)

Jordan, Clarence, *The Cotton Patch Version Of Luke And Acts*, and *The Cotton Patch Version Of Paul's Letters* (Association Press, New York, 1969)

Lacy, Mary Lou, *And God Wants People* (John Knox Press, Richmond, Va., 1962).

McFarland, John Robert, Article: "The Sermon Within the Context of Contemporary Worship" (*Pulpit Digest*—October, 1969)

Micks, Marianne H., *The Future Present* (Pulpit Book Club Selection, 400 Community Drive, Manhasset, New York, 11030, 1970)

Osborn, G. Edwin, *The Glory of Christian Worship* (Christian Theological Seminary Press, Indianapolis, Indiana, 1960)

Peterson, Wilferd A., *The Art of Living* (Simon and Schuster, N.Y., 1961)

Quoist, Michael, *Prayers of Life* (M. H. Gill, Dublin, Ireland, 1966)

Raines, Robert, *Creative Brooding* (Macmillan, New York, 1966)

———, *New Life in the Church*, Ibid

Randolph, David James, *Ventures In Worship* (Abingdon Press, Nashville, Tennessee, 1969)

Robinson, John A. T., *But That I Can't Believe* (New American Library, 1967)

———, *Liturgy Coming to Life* (Westminster Press, Philadelphia, Penna., 19107, 1960)

Services for the Church (8 booklets) (United Church of Christ, 1505 Rose St., Philadelphia, Penna., 19102)

Smallgried, Kay, *Spilled Milk: Litanies In Living* (Oxford University Press, New York, 1964)

Sunday Bulletins (United Methodist Church, San Luis Obispo, California)

Taylor, Michael, *Liturgical Renewal In The Christian Church* (Helicon Press, Baltimore, Maryland, 1967)

Teilhard de Chardin, Pierre, *Hymn of the Universe* (Harper & Row, New York, 1961)

Trueblood, Elton, *The Common Ventures of Life* (Harper & Row, 1940)

The Church at Worship in an Urban Age, By 12 San Francisco Area Ministers (Celebration West, 2735 MacArthur Blvd., Oakland, California, 94602)

Watkins, Keith, *Liturgies In A Time When Cities Burn* (Abingdon Press, Nashville, Tennessee, 1969)

Word Alive, An Anthology (Galaxy Press, New York)

Word and Action, New Forms of the Liturgy (Seabury Press, New York, 1969)

Words, Sheila D., *Youth Ventures Toward A Vital Church* (Abingdon Press, Nashville, Tennessee, 1965)

INDEX